Guns at Le Cateau
Two Accounts of the B.E.F. in the First World War

The Royal Regiment of Artillery at Le Cateau, 26 August, 1914

A. F. Becke

The Stand at Le Cateau, 26th August, 1914

C. de Sausmarez

LEONAUR

Guns at Le Cateau
Two Accounts of the B.E.F. in the First World War
The Royal Regiment of Artillery at Le Cateau, 26 August, 1914
by A. F. Becke
The Stand at Le Cateau, 26th August, 1914
by C. de Sausmarez

FIRST EDITION

First published under the titles
The Royal Regiment of Artillery at Le Cateau, 26 August, 1914
and
The Stand at Le Cateau, 26th August, 1914

Leonaur is an imprint of Oakpast Ltd

ISBN: 978-1-78282-184-7 (hardcover)
ISBN: 978-1-78282-185-4 (softcover)

http://www.leonaur.com

Publisher's Notes

Contents

Guns at Le Cateau

"*C'est avec d'artillerie qu'on fait la guerre*"—Napoleon.
(*Corr.* 11417—Posen, 8 December, 1806).

Preface

This study has been undertaken, first, to show officers of the regiment the use that will be made of their war diaries, and the nature of the information that is required for historical work; and, second, to encourage all officers, who were present at the action, to submit any further information that is in their possession. It is also hoped that it may prove of some instructional value.

I am indebted to the courtesy of the Historical Section, Committee of Imperial Defence, for permission to use the war diaries when writing this account.

I wish to record my indebtedness to my colleague Captain J. J. Bell, 20th Battalion, London Regiment, for his untiring assistance and advice; and to acknowledge most gratefully the valuable help given to me so freely by Captain C. T. Atkinson, O.U.O.T.C., Officer in Charge of the Historical Section (Military Branch), Committee of Imperial Defence.

A. F. Becke.

Public Record Office, W.C. 2.
August, 1918.

ERRATA

Maps 3 and 5
Since the blocks were made for the maps, it has been ascertained that the placing of the 41st Battery, R.F.A., is inaccurate.
Its correct position should be 900 yards east of that shown on maps 3 and 5. The battery was in action at the north-east corner of a small copse and face north-west.

Introduction

The more closely it is studied the more certain it becomes that the action fought by General Sir H. Smith-Dorrien and the troops under his command on August 26th, 1914, was not only a triumph for the British arms but had a most important bearing on the whole retreat. Indeed it is not too much to claim that future historians will pronounce Le Cateau to be one of the most important delaying actions recorded in history[1].

The time has come when the part played by the regiment on this critical day can be examined. It is impossible at this stage to give the Germans any information that can be of the slightest value to them[2]; on the other hand it is necessary to set down as soon as possible the story as far as it is known, so that survivors may be able to correct statements, placings of batteries, etc., which at present it is impossible to give more accurately from the data available. Any further delay will obviously make correction more difficult. once comparative accuracy is reached then the work will be made easy for the historian of this period of the regiment's history, and incidentally the production of the staff history of the war will be assisted materially when the time comes to write it.

At first sight it would appear that nothing further is required than a close study of the war diaries submitted periodically by each unit; but officers who have kept them know their shortcomings as well as those whose duty it is to work on them. Kept as they were amidst the confusion of a great retreat, by officers overcome by weariness, in several cases by junior officers who were the only survivors of historic

---

1. The present day popular view is simply expressed by Major Whitton in his book called *The Marne Campaign*. He writes "The British overwhelmed at Le Cateau". No statement could be more inaccurate.
2. The Germans remained on the field at the close of the action.

units that had suffered heavily in the fight, sometimes put together weeks afterwards, when memory was dulled by other events which had thronged thick and fast on top of one another, the wonder is not that there are omissions of important facts and misstatements about time, but that they do succeed generally in giving a wonderful picture of this strenuous and critical day.[3] But the diaries, even when they are first-hand evidence, are insufficient by themselves, and as far as possible they have been supplemented by statements from officers who were present at the engagement. If any other officers would communicate with the author any corrections about their own or neighbouring units, or supply any additional facts, they will be most gratefully received and recorded.[4]

3. It must be stated quite frankly that in very few diaries is a rough sketch, or tracing, appended to show the position in action occupied by the battery or brigade. Very few diaries give the ammunition expenditure. In hardly any case (except in the diaries of the R.H.A. Batteries) is a nominal role furnished of the officers serving with the battery, or brigade, when it landed in France. Many diaries are not even signed, and thus this means of identification of the battery commander is not available In other words, impressed by the necessity for Jacksonian secrecy, officers have too often carried it to excess. For instance, in one case an officer described the position of his battery as "In France". The probabilities were strongly in favour of the general accuracy of this maddening statement which the officer had the effrontery to label "confidential"! It is also most unfortunate that all batteries did not keep diaries, particularly for this early period. Valuable battery records are therefore missing for ever.

4. To prove the need for additional information to supplement the official diaries it is only necessary to quote in full two of the brigade diaries for 26th August 1914 (the names are purposely omitted to prevent identification). One runs:—"Retired all day covering rear guard of infantry. Came into action near —— and did a night march to ——" The other states:—"7 *a.m.* moved to —— found infantry engaged. All three batteries came into action and took part in the fighting all day. *6 p.m.* Fighting ceased. *7 p.m.* Retirement continued, arriving —— 2 a.m. 27th August." It is only fair to say that the original of the second diary was lost in the retreat and the description of the action was reconstructed from notes. Officers whose duty it is to keep the diary of the unit must remember that in labouring to be brief it is quite possible to become obscure. Everyone will agree that from official records it would take an experienced journalist to describe in detail the work of the two brigades in question. So far for obvious reasons, only officers in England and Switzerland have been asked for information.

Note.—The following abbreviations are used:—B.E.F., for British Expeditionary Force; G.H.Q , for General Head Quarters; C.R.A., for (Officer) Commanding Royal .Artillery (of a division); B.C., for Battery Commander; O.P., for Observation Post; B.A.C., for Brigade Ammunition Column; D.A.C., for Divisional Ammunition Column.

Roman Numerals are used for Artillery Brigades, and Arabic for Batteries.

Chapter 1.

Opening Events

(See Map I and Sketches A and F.)

Great Britain having declared War on Germany, on August 4, mobilisation was at once carried out; and shrouded in secrecy the small B.E.F. crossed over to France between August 9 and August 15.[1] In accordance with the plan arranged the B E.F. now trained northwards and on August 21 had assembled in the concentration area about Landrécies. On that day it advanced towards Mons forming practically the Left Wing of the French Armies m Northern France.

The results of our air reconnaissances on August 22 (see Sketch F) established the following facts—a heavy action was in progress along the Sambre near Charleroi, and the French had retired from their first position. Large German forces, well covered by cavalry divisions, were moving through Southern Belgium. Indeed they were in close proximity to the British Expeditionary Force, of which the Second Division had not yet come into line. The information indicated that the Germans had formed the ambitious plan of effecting the double envelopment of the French Fifth Army and the B.E.F.[2]

1. The first portion of the B.E.F., under the supreme command of Field-Marshal Sir John French, included the Cavalry Division (I., II., III., IV. Cavalry Brigades), V. Cavalry Brigade, First Corps (First and Second Divisions), Second Corps (Third and Fifth Divisions), with 4 Squadrons R.F.C. etc., also 6 battalions of line of communication and army troops, 4 of which were formed into the 19th Infantry Brigade. Strength about 90,000, with 334 guns (216 18-pdrs.; 72 4.5" hows.; 16 60-pdrs.; and 30 13-pdrs.)

2. The three German Armies which advanced against the V. French Army and the B.E.F. were:—The 3rd German Army (v. Hausen) which attacked the French right, advancing from the East against the line of the Meuse, from Givet to Namur, the 2nd German Army (v. Bülow) which advanced from the North and attacked the Sambre between Namur and Charleroi; and the 1st German Army (v. Kluck), whose mission was to envelop and overwhelm the B.E.F. In the 1st Army were included the II., III., IV., IV. Reserve, and IX. Corps.

On Sunday, August 23 , the Germans advanced against the B.E.F. and a general action commenced with dramatic suddenness along the line of the Canal. [3] Fighting was severe from Obourg westward, almost to Condé, the German attacks in massed formation being heavily punished by the rapid fire of the infantry outpost line. Through the lack, however, of any suitable positions from which the artillery could give support, the infantry had, towards evening, to retire to a second position farther to the Southward. Owing to the news received about 5 p.m. on August 23, concerning the situation of the French Armies on his right,[4] Field-Marshal Sir John French ordered a retirement of the B.E.F. which would otherwise have been exposed to an annihilating defeat in detail.[5]

On Monday, August 24, the retirement began. The First Corps, fell back south-westward of Maubeuge covered by the Second Corps, which at first had taken up a position along the line of the mining villages—Frameries—Wasmes—Dour—about three miles to the southward of its original position along the Mons Canal. Here the German advance was rudely checked and despite heavy fighting, which fell hardest on the Fifth Division, the Second Corps was withdrawn by nightfall and bivouacked in the. neighbourhood of Bavai. [6]

On the morrow the retirement was to be continued, the First Corps moving to the east of the Forest of Mormal and the Second Corps to the west. At this time Field-Marshal Sir John French contemplated fighting a delaying action in the neighbourhood of Le Cateau and some trenches were prepared to the west of that place and

---

3. In one unit, 2nd Duke of Wellington's Regiment (Fifth Division), the men had just returned from bathing in the bath-houses at the coal mines when 3 shells burst over the town (St. Ghislain).

4. The V. French Army had suffered a reverse at Charleroi and with their right (or E.) flank threatened no recovery was possible in the advanced position on the Sambre, therefore the *generalissimo* wisely decided to fall back until he could meet the crushing tide of the German advance with the certainty not only of staving it but of forcing it back.

5. The Royal Flying Corps observers had already brought in a considerable amount of information concerning the dispositions and movements of the German Army in Belgium. On this day, 24th August, an observer reported that he saw at 4.30 a.m. a heavy German column (possibly the leading division of the German IV Corps) moving S.W. between Ath and Peruwelz. This was verified about noon by another reconnaissance that was undertaken. The field marshal's decision to retire promptly from his exposed position was both sound and timely.

6. "Dour" will be the most suitable battle honour for the Germans to select in commemoration of this day's fighting.

south of the Cambrai *chaussée.*[7]

The forced marches from detrainment stations to the concentration area;[8] the constant digging to strengthen the positions; the heavy and continuous fighting against the great numerical superiority of the Germans; the disheartening change in the plan of operations; the retirement, for which the troops could not appreciate the necessity, as they had inflicted such heavy losses on the foe; the lack of rest; the disorganisation of the supply service, owing to the change of plan; (see note following), the great heat and the *paves*—all these things naturally were a great ordeal to all. On the comparatively large proportion of reservists present in the ranks, too little inured to physical exertions, the strain must have been tremendous. But the old regimental traditions stood the grim test and *esprit de corps* carried through many a worn-out man until the dawn broke on September 6, and the great advance began.[9]

Note. Taking the Fifth Division as a whole:—

Aug. 23rd—Supplies not distributed, as a retreat was ordered.

Aug. 24th—No distribution of supplies.

Aug. 25th—Lorries dumped supplies at Reumont; drawn by supply sections on arrival.

11 p.m., Aug. 26th—During a halt, 1 mile S. of Estrées, supplies were drawn direct from lorries.

In further illustration may be quoted the adventures of one unit of the Fifth Division—1/D.C.L.I.—Outpost duty on and defence of the Mons Canal from 1 p.m. 22nd, till 11 p.m. 23rd Aug. No rest on

---

7. Whereas some of the trenches near Audencourt proved of service on Aug. 26th, those on the spur nearer to Le Cateau were useless—being sited principally with the idea of avoiding damage to existing cultivation. Their position is indicated on Sketch B. No emplacements for guns have been traced.

8. 52 R.F.A. (XV. R.F.A. Brigade) with the Fifth Division, detrained at Le Cateau on Friday, 21st Aug., and marched to Dour which it reached the next day. The battery covered the 32 miles in loss than 24 hours and without any casualties.

9. It is 135 miles as the crow flies between Nimy (on the Canal N. of Mons) and Retal (S.E. of Paris), the two extreme points reached by the Third Division. This is equivalent in England to the distance between Westminster Bridge and Chesterfield (Derbyshire). Actually the distance marched was considerably greater. The 35th Heavy Battery, R.G.A., with the Second Division, records all its marches; and from Aug. 24th to Sept. 5th (both inclusive) it covered 208 miles. To this amount should be added 42 miles—its marches to the front on Aug. 22nd and 23rd, from Wassigny to Harveng.

night 23/24; rations failed on 23rd Aug. Outpost duty again on night 24/25 Aug.; neither officers nor men had eaten anything since 11 a.m. on that day.

At 5 a.m., 25th Aug. retirement continued the battalion furnishing the rear party until 2 p.m.; Le Cateau was reached at 6.30 p.m. The men were then served out with rations. The battalion was formed up ready to march again at 6.25 a.m. on 26th Aug.

In XXVIII. R.F.A. (with Fifth Division) on arrival at their bivouac S.W. of Le Cateau, on the night of the 25/26th, oats were issued. (More details are required about issues of food and forage, the artillery diaries being all strangely silent on this point.)

In "J" Battery, R.H.A. (Major Seligman) attached to the V. Cavalry Brigade, working with the First Corps, supplies did not arrive on 25th Aug., so a calf and a pig were killed. It is distressing to relate the reward of this display of initiative—the pig went bad!

In "I" Battery, R.H.A , rations were only issued on three occasions in ten consecutive days, commencing with 21st Aug. When describing the retreat an officer of the battery said, " I never knew that one could be so hungry and so tired and still be alive."

Meanwhile a welcome reinforcement reached the B.E.F.; for on this same day, August 24. the Fourth Division began to arrive to the west of Le Cateau, and on August 25, it moved out towards Solesmes to cover the withdrawal of the Second Corps and the 19th Infantry Brigades.

> Note.—At Le Cateau, on 25th Aug., the Fourth Division was deficient of its Heavy Battery and Divisional Ammunition Column. Its available complement of artillery was therefore only 72 guns—54 18-pdrs. and 18 4.5" howitzers.
>
> The Fourth Division was also without its Divisional Cavalry, Divisional Cyclists, Signal Company, R.E., Field Companies, R.E., Field Ambulances and Divisional Train. It fought and marched under considerable disadvantages.
>
> With the Sixth Division it was to form the Third Corps; but the Sixth Division did not arrive till mid-September, coming up on the Aisne. The Third Corps was not officially formed until Sept. 1st. during the retreat. Until then the Fourth Division manoeuvred under the commander of the Second Corps, who had obtained its co-operation on the battlefield of Le Cateau.
>
> At 7.45 a.m., on Aug. 25th. the G.O.C. Fourth Division in-

formed the commander of the Second Corps, " ... Have been ordered by Headquarters to report to you in order to assist you, if you require it ..." (G.G.3.).

CHAPTER 2

Retirement to the Le Cateau
Position
(Maps 1 and 5 and Sketches A and AA.)

As a result of the general south-westerly retirement on August 24, and the pressure on the left (west) flank, which fell on the Fifth Division, the Third Division passed behind the Fifth which had covered its retirement; and thus after this day their positions in the line are reversed—the Fifth being now to east, and the Third to west.[1] General Sir H. Smith-Dorrien [2] decided to retire his corps, screened by the cavalry division, at one bound to the Le Cateau position, the Fifth Division moving south along the straight Roman Road that runs past the west boundary of the Forest of Mormal, whilst the Third Division retired on Caudry in two columns, *via* Le Quesnoy and Solesmes. The Fourth Division moved out to Solesmes to cover this retirement.

That night (Tuesday, August 25) the force reached the following line:—

Fifth Division—East of Le Cateau—Troisvilles.
Third Division—Audencourt—Caudry.
Fourth Division—Ligny-Fontaine au Pire—Haucourt.[3]
19th Inf. Bde.—In Le Cateau and near Le Cateau Station.
The cavalry division was much split up, having its furthest detach-

---

1. They crossed back again during the retreat and resumed their original positions on 29th Aug., when S. of the Oise.
2. General Sir James Grierson, who went to France to command the Second Corps, died in the train between Rouen and Amiens on the way to the front, on Monday, 17th Aug. The command was then given to General Sir H. Smith-Dorrien, and he reached Bavai in the afternoon of Friday, 21st Aug.
3. This was only completed by the early a.m. of 26th Aug.

ments at Catillon and Viesly.[4]

On this same day the First Corps had been delayed and had not reached their allotted positions, actually halting for the night on the right bank of the Sambre to the south-east of the Forest of Mormal, between Le Grand Fayt-Dompierre-Landrécies and Noyelles. That evening the Germans [5] blundered on to the Guards' brigade at Landrécies and after a hot fight were repulsed.

Meanwhile, during the afternoon, the commander-in-chief decided that the action he had intended to fight with the two corps on August 26 must be deferred till later in the retreat, when some natural obstacle, like the Somme or Oise, should have been placed between the B.E.F. and the Germans; consequently on Aug. 25 he ordered that the retirement should be continued and that the B.E.F. was to march on August 26 to the line Busigny—Prémont—Beaurevoir—Le Catelet. In order to comply, orders were issued by the Second Corps at 10.15 p.m. for the force to continue the southward march, the Fourth Division starting at 7 a.m. and the Second Corps conforming to it.

It is now necessary to consider the state of affairs in the Second Corps on that Tuesday evening. There is no doubt that the long march performed on that day, especially that of the Fifth Division along the Roman Road, had proved most exhausting, particularly to the troops on rearguard duty. The constant checks and frequent deployments tried the men already wearied by three days spent in almost continuous marching, digging and fighting, and always on short rations. In particular the Fifth Division suffered most from the scorching heat of the day, passing as they did under the lee of the Forest of Mormal whose great trees[6] held off from the marching column any breeze there was, so that along that seven mile stretch the heat was almost suffocating.

In the Third Division the 7th Infantry Brigade, which acted as rearguard and was sharply engaged at Solesmes towards dusk, only reached Caudry at a very late hour and the men were very exhausted. The state of the infantry of the Second Corps on that Tuesday night, as well as the dispersed bivouacs occupied by the cavalry division, must have caused the commander on the spot to question the possibility of withdrawing

4. The H. Q. of the R.F.C. made the following changes of station in the early days:—Maubeuge (17th Aug.), Le Cateau (24th), S. Quentin (25th), La Fere (27th) and Compiègne (28th).

5. Probably part of the IX. German Corps.

6. There was a forest on this same site in Roman times. In 1914 about four-fifths of the total area was covered by big trees—beech, oak and hornbeam.

any further on the next day and of covering the movement adequately with his slender force of cavalry, without first of all administering a severe check to the pursuing German Army. Knowing the British soldier so well he realised that the troops would have attempted another 20 mile march on the morrow but such an effort must have been too costly in stragglers to face, if it could be avoided.

Unless the enemy were delayed, how could the First Corps, whose nearest troops at Landrécies were 7 miles away to the north-east of Le Cateau, ever effect a retirement through Guise.[7] Again if the Germans were not roughly handled and checked on August 26 they would be able to attack on August 27 with far greater advantages than they possessed on the 26th, when the long bound in retirement—from Bavai to the Le Cateau position—had undoubtedly spread-eagled the pursuers.[8]

General Sir Horace Smith-Dorrien rose superior to the occasion; during the night August 25/26 he decided that the Second Corps must stand and fight on the Le Cateau position and he issued orders accordingly to his troops, taking over as well the cavalry division, the Fourth Division,[9] and the 19th Infantry Brigade [10] who were on the ground. In the early morning of August 26 he telephoned his decision to G.H.Q. at St. Quentin[11];[12]

---

7. For situation at night see Sketch AA.

8. A German Corps had been allowed to rest after passing Dour on 24th Aug., whilst a fresh one moved to the front and continued the pursuit. On 26th Aug. the resting corps was suddenly called out and pushed forward in motor-lorries to take part in the action at Le Cateau.

9. The message received at 7.20 a.m. by the Fourth Division is still available among the Appenices to Vol. 1. of its G.S. Diary; it runs as follows:—To Fourth Division. G.W. 1 (Aug. 26). From information received from the cavalry it has been found necessary to remain in our present position. The Second Corps is talking up a position from Reumont-Troisvilles-Audencourt-Caudry Station. Sir Horace Smith-Dorrien hopes that you will hold the ground on his left as far as Haucourt. From Second Corps Bertry.

10. G.H.Q. O.O.8 of 25th Aug. (issued at 1 p.m.) placed the 19th Inf. Bde. under the orders of the Second Corps.

11. F.S. Regus., Part 1., Chapter 2, para. 13. states very clearly the latitude allowed to a subordinate with regard to the precise execution of the orders given to him by his superior.

12. At 5 a.m. August 26th. the following message was sent from the Second Corps to G.H.Q.:—"G. 368. Inform French Cavalry Corps that Second Corps is not retiring today, and ask for their co-operation on our left flank."

At the same hour the Second Corps informed the Fifth Division:—"G. 367. The 19th Infantry Brigade is placed under your orders."

CHAPTER 3

R.A. Second Corps on Tuesday, August 25

(See Map 5).

(A) Fifth Division.

The Divisional Artillery, Fifth Division, retired with their division and bivouacked alongside the Roman Road to the north of Reumont. XV R.F.A. (11, 52 and 80 R.F.A .) with 61 (hows.) R.F.A. (detached from VIII R.F.A.) had been attached to the rearguard (14th Infantry Brigade) and did not get in until dusk (about 7 p.m.) after a trying march that had lasted since 4 a.m.[1] One piece of good fortune had attended 61 on the only occasion when it fired on this day. When engaging some concealed German guns, a shrapnel shell from one of the howitzers burst over a viaduct, destroying a company of German infantry who were engaged in crossing it at that precise moment. There is a certain grim satisfaction in recalling that the shell was off the line.

52 R.F.A. worked with the rear battalion of the rear guard and the battery came into action south of Bavai to cover the exits from the town. Whilst in this position some German cavalry were seen and successfully engaged. In the long march back to Reumont along the Roman Road, the country being very difficult and the only possible position being on the road itself, the B.C. kept a section with the rear party. These two guns were unlimbered repeatedly, coming into ac-

---

1. In 61 R.F.A. the horses, many of whom were remounts, were showing signs of the continuous work and scanty food. On 24th and 25th they had only one feed of corn; stocks of oats being used when available. During the retirement the horses seem to have been kept going by using the oat-straw, of which luckily there was an abundance.

tion behind the crest of every rise, but the Germans did not press and no target appeared. Although the battalion (l/D. C.L.I.) on rear party was relieved by another battalion (l/E. Surr. R.) of the 14th Infantry Brigade, when about half the distance had been covered, nevertheless the battery was not changed. 52 reached its bivouac to the north of Reumont at about 7 p.m., and on arrival the men were fortunate enough to get a hot meal.[2]

No orders for August 26 were issued to XV. R.F.A. when it arrived in bivouac, and the late hour prevented the brigade commander from carrying out any reconnaissance of the ground in his vicinity. During the night (at 1.15 a.m.) orders were received to continue the retirement and XV. was to be ready to move off at 3.30 a.m. with the 14th Infantry Brigade.

108 Heavy Battery had bivouacked at Wargnies overnight (24/25); to rejoin the column and reach Reumont necessitated a march of 25 miles—a very long one for a Heavy Battery at any time, especially so soon after mobilisation. On arrival in bivouac the battery replenished its ammunition that evening.

XXVII and VIII (Hows.) R.F.A., having marched fairly high up m the main body, were in earlier and had a less trying march than the units before mentioned.

XXVIII also retired with the division but, before arrival in arrival in bivouac, took up and entrenched a covering position north of Montay.[3] Just before sunset the brigade was hurriedly withdrawn, but did not reach the bivouac near Reumont until 11.30 p.m., owing to a bad block in the village of Montay which occasioned some hours delay.

123 R.F.A. had become detached from XXVIII in the retirement from Dour on August 24, and marched on August 25 with XXVII; thus it preceded XXVIII in the marching column and was not deflected from the road at Montay.[4] It arrived at the Reumont bivouac

---

2. No rations had been issued to the battery either on 23rd or on 24th and the iron rations were then opened. On the march into Bavai, early on the 25th, 52 passed the 2/Manchester R. (14th Inf. Bde.) who stated they were without food. Each man of the battery gave up two of his biscuits to them.

3. The 2/Suffolk R. and 2/Manchester R, 14th Bde., who had been with the rearguard, also extended on this position, allowing the other 2 battalions of this brigade (1 E. Surrey R. and 1/D. C.L.I.) to pass through and proceed to Le Cateau.

4. To take the place of 123, 11 R.F.A. of XV, remained with XXVIII when the position at Montay was occupied. 11 R.F.A. finally bivouacked with its brigade to the N.W of Reumont, but did not reach the bivouac until very late at night

about 5 p.m., and here the whole Brigade was finally reassembled that night. XXVIII B.A.C. had undergone a different experience. Marching from Wargnies at 1.30 a.m. it attempted to regain the marching column of the Fifth Division, but was cut off by the Flank Guard of the Third Division and marched with it for some time. Then gradually working across country it reached the neighbourhood of Reumont about 5 p.m. As far as can be ascertained all the B.A.Cs. bivouacked near Reumont on the night 25/26 August. The Fifth Division D.A.C. retired to Reumont with the division and bivouacked there; some time early next morning detached portions of Nos. 2 and 3 sections appear to have rejoined the column.

The C.R.A's H.Q. were in Reumont and in the same village were situated the H.Q. of the Fifth Division.

Thus on this night the artillery of the Fifth Division was concentrated once more under its C.R.A. Considering the difficult nature of the retirement on August 24, the pressure applied to the Fifth Division on that day, the somewhat scattered bivouacs occupied that evening, and the march of the Third Division cutting across the line of retreat of the Fifth Division, this was in itself a considerable feat.

Meanwhile, whilst marching southwards, orders had reached the column that the force was to turn about on August 26 and fight on a selected position. Thus the rare opportunity was given of studying the ground from the hostile point of view, and this was seized by the C.R.A. On reaching the line, which it was intended to hold, he rode over his section of it himself, but unfortunately heavy rain commenced falling about 5 p.m. thus obscuring the view. Consequently he arranged with his brigade commanders to carry out a detailed reconnaissance at dawn (about 1 a.m.).

All the units occupied sodden, cheerless bivouacs in a drenching rain that lasted from 5 p.m. till midnight when at last it ceased. It was a dismal end to one of the longest days.

(B) Third Division.

Generally speaking the artillery of the Third Division were not quite so highly tried on August 24 and 25 as that belonging to the Fifth Division. Their march was more varied than the Fifth Division's along the dead straight Roman Road which presented a *vista* that appeared to be never ending. There was no forest, like Mormal, to complicate the move and act as a suffocating blanket alongside the line of march. A part of the division (8th Infantry Brigade and XL R.F.A.)

had actually bivouacked at Amfroipret well on the line of retirement. The artillery also seems to have been less scattered than was the case in the Fifth Division.

Attached to the rearguard (7th Infantry Brigade) were XLII and XXX (Hows) R.F.A., but except in the neighbourhood of Solesmes (about 5 to 5. 30 p.m.) there seems to have been no firing. In the retirement from Solesmes 41 R.F.A. became detached from its brigade[5] and then it accompanied the original rear party (2/R. Irish Rifles) marching *via* Montay—Le Cateau—Reumont and Bertry. They passed the last named place about a.m. on August 26.

The rest of XLII reached Caudry about 11 p.m. and billeted there. XXX (Hows.) R.F.A. were less fortunate, they did not reach Caudry until midnight and had to bivouac in the wet streets.

XXIII R.F.A. in the main column, starting at 4 a.m., reached Troisvilles at 5.30 p.m. Realising that an action was to be fought on that ground next day, the brigade commander reconnoitred the portion allotted to his brigade and his batteries bivouacked in rear of it ready to occupy it at daylight. It had been decided that two sections should occupy a forward position in rear of the infantry firing line, from which the valleys and covered approaches running south from Inchy could be swept with fire. These forward positions were selected on arrival and 107 and 108 proceeded to prepare entrenchments for a section from each battery. In the case of the forward section of 108 the pits (as well as two dummies) were dug in the dark in a root-field between 8 and 10.30 p.m. 109 also reconnoitred the position that the battery would occupy on the morrow.

XL R.F.A.[6] reached Caudry about 4 p.m. and billeted to the E. of the town; with it was XL B.A.C.

48 Heavy Battery, on arrival in the neighbourhood of Troisvilles, occupied a rough defensive position to the west of the village, bivouacking there for the night.

The Third D.A.C. had marched at 2 a.m., it parked to the west of Bertry, being complete with the exception of a few wagons.[7]

The C.R.A's H.Q. were in Bertry, which also contained the H.Q.

---

5. Unfortunately the appendix containing the report of 41 on its work this day was never sent in with the brigade diary and cannot be traced.

6. XL had had difficulty the previous night at Amfroipret with its supplies. They had been dumped in the vicinity of the bivouac, but then it was found that no wagon was available to fetch them; an exasperating situation. Fortunately they were eventually sent up by a motor-lorry.

7. They were in Le Cateau. They marched to rejoin very early next morning.

of the Third Division as well as that of the Second Corps.

Thus in the Third Division the artillery was well in hand at night, the ground had been reconnoitred and in the two important cases entrenchments had actually been dug for the advanced sections that were to co-operate closely with the infantry defence.

Here as with the Fifth Division, as evening fell, the weather turned cold and wet; but this was not sufficient to prevent the earliest arrivals from making the most of the short time at their disposal.

(C) Fourth Division.

This Divisional Field Artillery[8] had a very different experience. The batteries spent August 21 in the train on the way to the front, detraining well to the south of what became, on August 20, the battlefield of Le Cateau. During August 25, XIV, XXIX, XXXII, and XXXVII (Hows.) concentrated in the neighbourhood of Briastre; as they gradually finished their several detrainments, they made a rapid march to the front to join the infantry of the Fourth Division, who were waiting in the neighbourhood of Solesmes ready to take the pressure off the retiring troops.

At night the Divisional Field Artillery concentrated at Ligny, and the B.A.C's also seem to have been in the same neighbourhood. XXXII having been on rearguard with the 10th Infantry Brigade reached Ligny much later than the rest.[9]

The C.R.A's H.Q. were at Haucourt, at which place were also the H.Q. of the Fourth Division.

The entry of the Fourth Division into active operations had been uncomfortable. The delay at home whilst the other divisions left, then the concentration at Harrow, the hurried and crowded passage across, the equally hurried and crowded train journey to the north of France, the swift detrainment followed by a rapid march into action, had imposed a severe trial on all. But on the night of August 25/26 the C.R.A. had his brigades well under his hand, though in the existing circumstances it had not been possible to make any reconnaissance of

8. The adventures of 31st Heavy Battery are rather striking:—Arriving at Boulogne at 1.30 p.m. on 24th Aug. it landed there, only to re-embark the next day. On 26th Aug. it sailed for Havre, disembarking the same day. On Sept. 2nd it re-embarked once more; sailed on the 3rd Sept.; reached S. Nazaire on the 5th, disembarked the same day: finally it entrained for the front on the 7th, when the advance had already begun. The Fourth D.A.C. which had arrived at Havre at noon 24th Aug., entrained for S. Quentin on 25th, and detrained at that place dining the morning of 26th August.

9. The batteries seem to have passed the rest of the night halted in the road.

this section of the field.

(D) Royal Horse Artillery.

III R.H.A.

"D" R.H.A., although nominally attached to the I Cavalry Brigade apparently was never in touch with them all day. At night "D" reached Catillon with the III Cavalry Brigade and portions of I and II; and there it bivouacked, the men sleeping on the road.[10] "E" R.H.A.[11] passed through Le Quesnoy and Romeries during the retirement and finally halted for the night to the south-west of Le Cateau with the I Cavalry Brigade (see "L" below).

VII R.H.A.

"L" R.H.A.,[12] starting at 1 a.m. with the II Cavalry Brigade, reached Vertain about 5 p.m. Here there was a great congestion of troops, including French Territorials, and a halt was made to allow the troops to get clear. At dark the retirement was resumed again, "L" Battery now being in rear of the column. Possibly darkness saved this part of the force when passing through a sunken road with German infantry only a short quarter of a mile behind it. In the early morning "L" and the I Cavalry Brigade bivouacked in a field in the Fifth Divisional Area.

"I" R.H.A. Unfortunately no diary was kept for this battery but as far as possible the omission has been made good from private sources, so that the war services of this magnificent battery—the troop ever associated in the minds of all gunners with the names of Norman Ramsay and Fuentes d'Onoro—may be chronicled to swell its previous record. Within 10 years of its formation, in 1805, the war services of "I" Troop numbered 60; they ring like trumpet calls from the past—

10. The Right Section (Lieut. Watson) after having been detached to a flank got separated from the battery and did not rejoin for a considerable time. The story of this section would be very acceptable. Eventually Lieut. Watson and his section joined up with "I" R.H.A. during the retreat after Le Cateau. The 8 gun battery thus formed was reorganised by Major W. G. Thompson into a brigade of two 4 gun Horse Artillery Batteries.

11. It appears that "E" fired the first round from our artillery in this war. On Aug. 22nd at 10.30 a.m. the battery was in action near Braye (see map 1), and it opened on some German guns that were shelling Peronnes; but the range was excessive and "E" soon ceased fire.

12. Fine as the record of "L" R.H.A. had been in H.E.I.C.S. yet it is certain that it had never shot with more deadly effect than it did on the previous day (24th Aug.) at Audregnies. Though "D", "B" and 119th R.F.A. co-operated in this fight, "L" had been the battery that was chiefly responsible tor taking the sting out of the outflanking attack of a German corps which threatened the left flank of the Fifth Division in its retirement from the Dour position.

"Busaco"; "Redinha"; "Fuentes d'Onoro"; "Badajoz"; Salamanca"; "Vittoria"; "San Sebastian"; "Waterloo".

On August 25 "I" retired from the neighbourhood of Saultain with the IV Cavalry Brigade. When north of Haussy the column was shelled from the north-west and "I" came into action at once against the German guns. The battery had not fired previously in the campaign. Later on the column retired to Solesmes and at 5 p.m. "I" unlimbered again, immediately to the north of the town. From this position the battery fired .10 rounds against German artillery in action to the north and north-west. The German fire was quite ineffective—very short. When ordered to retire and billet at Beaumont, "I" had to move through S. Python, as Solesmes was blocked by troops.[13] In passing through Viesly "I" got attached to XLII R.F.A. of the Third Division and moved with it to Caudry, reaching there between 10 and 11 p.m. "I" billeted in a square on the western face of Caudry. It was no longer in touch with the IV Cavalry Brigade.

The Royal Horse Artillery was necessarily much split up. During the retreat, the Batteries were used as they were required. Moreover, their scattered bivouacs on the night of August 25/26 were not serious in view of the fact that a delaying action was to be fought on the morrow, because for that purpose Field Artillery and Heavy Batteries were primarily required; and, when the time came to withdraw, the Horse Artillery would be well in hand for use directly the necessity arose for the employment of more mobile guns. What was more important, as the left flank had extra protection—Sordet's cavalry and French horse artillery[14]—was that guns might be required to cover the open right flank of the Second Corps and to secure the spur to the S. of Le Cateau, near which our infantry had halted on the Tuesday night; and fortunately nearly three-fourths of the Royal Horse Artillery would be available for this task from an early hour, for practically three of the Batteries had bivouacked beyond the right flank or in the Fifth Divisional Area.

---

13. Shortly afterwards the German guns lengthened their range and set Solesmes on fire.

14. On the afternoon of 25th Aug. an officer of XL. B.A.C. saw Sordet's cavalry marching W. along the Cambrai *chaussée*.

CHAPTER 4

The Order of Battle of the R.A. Second Corps on August 26

Now that the situation on the Tuesday night has been appreciated, as well as the disposition of the available artillery on that same night, it will be wise to summarize the units present on the ground, giving as far as possible their commanders.

ORDER OF BATTLE OF ROYAL ARTILLERY AT LE CATEAU.

Royal Horse Artillery[1] with the Cavalry Division.
C.R.H.A.[2,4]
Colonel B. F. Drake.[3]

III R.H.A.[2,4] (Lieut.-Col. R. W. Breeks).
"D"[2] (Major G. Gillson).
"E"[2] (Major A. B. Forman).
III R.H.A., B.A.C. (Capt. W. S. D. Craven).

VII R.H.A. (Lieut.-Col. J. F. N. Birch).
"I"[4] (Major W. G. Thompson).
"L"[2,4] (Major the Hon. W. D. Sclater-Booth).
VII R.H.A., B.A.C.[2] (Capt. C. D. Uniacke).

---

1. (Throughout list), the five R.H.A. Batteries—"D", "E", "I", "J" and "L"—that went to France with the original B.E.F. were made up, in personnel and guns, by other R.H.A. Batteries. They took no remounts or reservists with them.
2. (Throughout list), diaries are available for these units.
3. Lt.-Col. H. r. Dawson, R.A. and Major E. Benson, R.A., kindly gave me considerable assistance in compiling the nominal roll of the commanders of the various units.
4. (Throughout list), statements have been received from officers belonging to these units.

Number of guns with the Cavalry Division—4 Batteries, or 24 13-pdrs.

Divisional Artillery—Fifth Division.

C.R.A.[2,4,5]

Brig.-Genl. J. E. W. Headlam, C.B., D.S.O.

XV[2,4] (Lieut.-Col. C. F. Stevens).

11[4] (Major P. W. B. Henning).

52[2,4] (Major A. C. R. Nutt).

80[2,4] (Major R. A. Birley).

XV B.A.C. (Capt. W. G. Curling).

XXVII[2] (Lieut.-Col. W. H. Onslow).

119 (Major E. W. Alexander).

120 (Major C. S. Holland, killed at Mons, Aug. 23.).

121 (Major C. N. B. Ballard).

XXVII B.A.C. (Capt. D. K. Tweedie).

XXVIII[2,4] (Lieut.-Col. E. C. Cameron).

122 [4] (Major G. H. Sanders).

123 [4] (Major G. H. W. Bayley).

124 [4] (Major G. R. V. Kinsman)

XXVIII B.A.C.[2] (Capt. J. F. P. Thorburn).

VIII (Hows.),[2] (Lieut.-Col. E. J. Duffus).

37 [4] (Major E. H. Jones).

61 [2] (Major F. A. Wilson, D.S.O.).

65 [2] (Major J. E. C. Livingstone Learmonth).

VIII (Hows.) B.A.C. (Capt. I. D. Vernon).

108 Heavy Battery,[2] R.G.A. (60-pdrs) (Major C. de Sausmarez, D.S.O.).

Fifth Divisional Ammunition Column[2] (Lt.-Col. E. P. England).

Number of guns with Fifth Division—13 Batteries, or 52, 18-pdrs.[6]; 18, 4.5" hows.; and 1, 60-pdrs. Total—74.

Divisional Artillery—Third Division.

C.R.A.[2]

Brig.-Genl. F. D. V. Wing, C.B

XXIII [2] (Lieut.-Col. A. T. Butler).

5. The wagon in which this diary was carried was blown to pieces by a shell at Reumont on August 26th. The C.R.A. rewrote the description of the fighting, at Mons and Le Cateau, whilst the division was on the Aisne.

6. Two 18-pdrs. of 120 were lost on 23rd Aug.

107 [4] (Major L. J. Hext).
108 [4] (Major H. E. Carey).
109 [2],[4] (Major S. F. Metcalfe).
XXIII B.A.C. (Capt. H. W. Atchison).

XL [2] (Lieut.-Col. R. J. G. Elkington).
6 (Major E. W. S. Brooke).
23 (Major C. St. M. Ingham).
49 (Major J. S. Maidlow, killed at Mons, Aug. 23.).
XL B.A.C.[4] (Capt. the Hon. H. E. Thellusson).

XLII [4] (Lieut.-Col. G. H. Geddes).
29 (Major A. B. Bethell).
41[4] (Major T. Bruce).
45 (Major N. Gray, wounded at Mons, Aug. 24.).
XLII B.A.C. (Capt. D. le P. Trench).

XXX (Hows.)[2] (Lieut.-Col. W. C. Staveley).
128 (Major W. Strong).
129 (Major L. T. Ash worth).
130 (Major G. J. C. Stapylton, killed at Solesmes, Aug. 25.).
XXX (Hows.) B.A.C. (Capt. M. Muirhead).

48 Heavy Battery, R.G.A.,[2] (60-pdrs.) (Major C. F. Phipps).
Third Divisional Ammn. Column. [2] (Lieut.-Col. C. H. Ford).
Number of guns with Third Division—13 Batteries, or 54, 18-pdrs.; 18, 4.5" hows.; and 1, 60-pdrs. Total—76.

Divisional Artillery—Fourth Division.
C.R.A.[2]
Brig.-Genl. G. F. Milne, C.B., D.S.O.

XIV[2] (Lieut. -Col. C. M. Ross-Johnson, D.S.O.)
39 (Major E. S. E. W. Eardley-Russell, M.V.O.)
68 (Major W. A. Short),
88 (Major R. England, killed at Le Cateau, Aug. 26.).
XIV B. A. C. (Capt. E. W. M. Browne).

XXIX[2] (Lieut.-Col. H. E. Stockdale).
125 (Major H. G. Lloyd).
126 (Major R. A. G. Wellesley).
127 (Major E. W. Spedding).
XXIX B.A.C. (Capt. R. G. Maturin, D.S.O.)

XXXII[2];[4] (Lieut.-Col. M. J. MacCarthy).
27[4] (Major H. E. Vallentin).
134 (Major H. Ward).
135[4] (Major G. H. Liveing).
XXXII B.A.C. (Capt. J. Carruthers, M.V.O.)

XXXVII (Hows.) [2];[4] (Lieut.-Col. C. Battiscombe).
31 (Major D. H. Gill).
35 (Major H. A. Koebel).
55 (Major G. N. Cartwright).
XXXVII (Hows.) B.A.C. (Capt. H. M. Ballingall).

Number of guns with the Fourth Division[7]—12 Batteries, or 54,. 18-pdrs.; and 18, 4.5" hows. Total—72.

Thus the 42 Batteries available for the action on Aug. 26 were:
4 Batteries, Royal Horse Artillery.
36 Batteries, Royal Field Artillery (27 being 18-pdrs., and 9 4.5" hows.); and 2 Heavy Batteries, Royal Garrison Artillery.
In detail the guns were distributed as follows:—

	Cav. Divn.	Fifth Divn.	Third Divn.	F'rth Divn.	Total
13-pdrs.	24	—	—	—	24
18 "	—	52	54	54	160
4.5" hows.	—	18	18	18	54
60-,pdrs.	—	4	4	—	8
				Grand Total	246[8]

"D", "E" and "I", R.H.A. are direct descendants of three "Waterloo Troops"—Webber Smith's troop, Sir R. Gardiner's troop, and Bull's troop. (*The British Artillery at Waterloo*). "D" has also the honour of being one of the 4 original R.H.A. troops, although it was not formed until 1794. The above note must not be misunderstood; it is no attempt to compare the importance of the action of Le Cateau with the crushingly decisive Battle of Waterloo.

7. 31 Heavy Battery, R.G.A. (Major & Bt. Lt. Col. G. McK. Franks) and the Fourth Divisional Ammn. Col. (Lieut.-Col. H. Biddulph) were neither of them present on the battlefield of Le Cateau. Diaries are available for both of these units.

8. At Waterloo on June 18th, 1815, there were 156 guns in the Duke of Wellington's force, organised in 14 troops of Horse Artillery and 18 Field Brigades (all nationalities). The Royal Artillery was represented on that day by 8 troops, Royal Horse Artillery (42 guns and 6 howitzers) and 5 Field Brigades R.A. (27 guns and 3 howitzers)—total 78. (*Napoleon and Waterloo*, II., 35,36.)

CHAPTER 5

The Action of Le Cateau
Wednesday, August 26.

1. GENERAL SITUATION AT DAWN.
(See Maps 1 and 5 and Sketch B.)

There is no doubt that the German Army had followed close on the heels of General Sir H. Smith-Dorrien's corps and that the pursuers halted in fairly close contact with it. This fact, coupled with the difficulty that the very scattered cavalry division would experience in covering any further withdrawal and the obvious exhaustion of the three divisions now halted on the line Le Cateau—Caudry—Haucourt, had made it quite clear to the corps commander on the spot that, unless his troops could continue the retirement during the night, a serious action could not be avoided without running too great a risk of jeopardising the safety of the whole B.E.F. That further immediate withdrawal was quite out of the question was settled at a conference held at 2 a.m. at Corps H.Q. at Bertry.[1]

Shortly after dawn it also became certain that no co-operation could be expected from the First Corps, which, as well as being behind time, had had a very disturbed night, its further retreat being complicated by the presence of Germans at the edge of the Forest of Mormal on the left bank of the Sambre.

Consequently in the early morning the G.O.C. Second Corps issued orders for his whole available force to take up a position on the line Le Cateau—Quarries—Moulin d'Esnes,[2] and this position was to

1. Present at this half-hour's conference were G.O.C. Second Army Corps, and his G.S.O. 1: G.O.C. Cavalry Division. with his G.S.O. 1 and D.A.A. & Q.M.G., as well as the G. O.C. Third Division. (Diary of D.A.A. & Q.M.G., Cav. Divn.)
2. This place is often called "Mont d'Esnes". The mistake is easy to understand directly the Cambrai Sheet of the 1/80,000 map is consulted.

be held at all costs.

It will be convenient to take a brief glance at the battlefield and at the approximate strength of the two opposing forces, before considering in detail the part played by the Royal Regiment of Artillery on this day.

2. THE BATTLEFIELD
(See Map 5.)

From flank to flank, from the big spur to the north-east of Le Cateau on the one hand, through Troisvilles, Audencourt, and Caudry, to Esnes on the other, the selected position measured about thirteen miles, (see note following). This was to be held by the Fourth, Third, and Fifth Divisions . The Fifth Division on the right, holding from Le Cateau spur to Troisvilles (both inclusive) about four and a half miles; the Third Division in the centre, from Troisvilles (exclusive) to Caudry (inclusive) about four miles; and the Fourth Division on the left, from Caudry (exclusive) to Esnes (inclusive) about four and a half miles.

Note:—Some other frontages that are interesting to compare are:—

Waterloo, 1815, frontage 3 miles, held by the Duke of Wellington's Army. 67,000 strong, and 156 guns; of the 50,000 infantry, 15,000 were British and 5,000 were King's German Legion. (*Napoleon & Waterloo* ii.)

Weissenberg, 1870, a delaying action, the French held a front of 2½ miles with 5,200 rifles. 900 sabres. 12 guns, and 6 *mitrailleuses*. The available German force was 40,000 rifles, 3,000 sabres, and 144 guns; not more than half were engaged .

Gravelotte, 1870, 140,000 French and 456 guns held a position 9 miles in length.

R. Yalu, 1904, a delaying action, the Russians held a front of 12 miles, from An-tung—Chin-Kou, with 13,000 bayonets, 640 scouts, 48 guns and 8 m. guns. At *Liao Yung*, 1904, the Russian "Advanced position", 15½ miles in length, was held by 158.000 men (128,000 being infantry) with 36 howitzers, 28 siege guns and 609 field guns.

The battlefield is situated in the chalk country of Northern France, though between Le Cateau and Cambrai the chalk really forms the foundation and only crops out in the valleys, where the overlying *strata* have been removed by the action of the streams. The greater part of the field is covered with a fine grained yellow loam, its depth varying from a mere coating to a layer several feet thick; it is generally regarded as wind-borne, in other words a dust. Wherever it was encountered it probably proved easy to dig in, even with the "grubber."

At the time of the action the district was covered principally with corn-fields, but the corn was nearly all cut and stood in the fields in stooks; whilst scattered over the open but undulating landscape were patches of beet and clover-fields. The only restriction to the free movement of all arms was an occasional wire fence.

A feature of the landscape near the centre was a solitary, tall tree standing on the south bank of the hollow road to the east of Troisvilles (the *Arbre* of the 1/80,000 map). As this landmark would have been of use to the enemy, an unsuccessful attempt was made to cut it down before the action opened, great care having to be taken that the southerly wind did not cause the tree to fall into the cutting and thus prevent its use as a lateral covered way. The trunk, however, proved to be too thick and it was only half cut through when firing opened.

Most of the roads were sunken where they crossed the spurs, the cuttings being shallow trenches varying from three feet to six feet in depth; in other words they were ready for occupation by troops acting on the defensive wherever they happened to face in the required direction. Many proved suitable for use as communication trenches as well as providing shielded points of vantage that could be employed as observation posts and headquarters.

The rolling, billowy nature of the country and the numerous deep valleys, made the position one that was difficult to defend, as an assailant could approach quite close to many parts of the line before his advance could be observed and effective fire brought to bear on him.

The spur to the east of Le Cateau, once it passed definitely into German hands, would facilitate the envelopment of the right flank and would endanger the retreat. Whilst the occupation by the Germans of the long spur which runs to the north of the Warnelle Ravine must prejudice the defence of the left flank section of the line.

The villages situated on the field were strongly built. They were calculated to give ample cover from field-gun shrapnel, a point entirely in the German favour, but there was no time to prepare those held by the II Corps to withstand the effects of a heavy bombardment with high explosive.

Generally speaking the gun positions were more suitable for an assailant and particularly for an assailant who happened to be in a crushing numerical superiority. His guns could unlimber at starting on a wide arc where it was almost impossible to locate them and knock them out, except with Heavy Batteries—and only two of the latter were available. Then having subjected the guns of the defence to a heavy converging fire some of the German batteries could close up, covered by the fire of the others, and from these forward positions cover the advance of the rest of their artillery and prepare the final assault of their infantry.

But there were other grave disadvantages, one was that both flanks of the position were in the air; another that the line of retreat for the Fifth Division—the Roman Road to S. Quentin—ran in a south-westerly direction across the rear of the position and this would probably lead to tremendous confusion when the time came to retire and troops, transport, and ammunition columns all came crowding back on it at the close of the day.

Nevertheless, whatever its defects, it was necessary to hold the Le Cateau position at this juncture; no further retirement could be made at the moment, for the pursuit of the German Army had to be stopped once and for all. At any rate the position would suffice for that task and General Sir Horace Smith-Dorrien did not hesitate to take the responsibility in ordering its immediate occupation.

3. THE OPPOSING FORCES.

The Second Corps and attached troops that came under General Sir H. Smith-Dorrien's command on August 26 were:—

The Cavalry Division, Third, Fourth, and Fifth Divisions, and 19th Infantry Brigade. In other words:—12 Cavalry Regiments, and 2 Squadrons Divisional Cavalry; 40 Infantry Battalions; with 246 guns, and 90 machine guns at most.[3]

On the German side no less than four corps of the I German Army have beep identified as being engaged at Le Cateau on August 26—the II, III, IV and IV Reserve; and there were probably three Cavalry Divisions. Consequently the Germans had available for the action: at least—12 Cavalry Regiments, as well as 32 Squadrons, Di-

---

3. In the original B.E.F. each Cavalry Regiment and each Infantry Battalion had 2 machine guns. There were no other machine gun organisations in existence at that time. At Mons, 23rd and 24th Aug., several of our machine guns had been destroyed by gun-fire.

The Fourth Division was without its Divisional Cavalry & Signal Section on August 26th.

visional Cavalry; 102 Infantry Battalions (exclusive of Pioneers); with more than 600 guns; and about 240 machine guns.[4]

So far as any military undertaking can be made a matter of accurate forecast and calculation, the German Army was certain to overwhelm the heavily outnumbered British force that faced them undismayed on that August morning, calm in the assurance that at least they would render a good account of themselves, and glad that they were to change the disheartening *rôle* of retreat for the active one of hammer.

As the result proves the Germans have little they can boast about concerning the achievement of their desire on August 26.

---

4. This estimate of German machine guns must be taken as the minimum number that were present on August 26th. There is a mass of evidence, given in the diaries and by officers present at the action, that the Germans had an overwhelming superiority in machine guns and handled them very boldly.

CHAPTER 6

The Action of Le Cateau
(Continued)

The Artillery at Dawn, Wednesday, August 26.

(a) Fifth Division—(See Map 2 and Sketch B.)

During the night of August 25/26 orders had reached the C.R.A. that the retirement was to be continued; consequently XXVIII R.F.A. had been detailed for work with the rearguard on August 26.[1] XXVIII accordingly moved north along the Roman Road, about 3 a.m., to take up a rearguard position m the neighbourhood of Pont des Quatre Vaux so as to assist the 13th Infantry Brigade to cover the withdrawal of the Fifth Division from its bivouacs around Reumont, and this position was to be maintained until 11 a.m.[2]

The morning broke fine but cool and very misty, and thus the selection of this rearguard position was very difficult.

Just before dawn (about 2.30 a.m.), as a preliminary measure, the Fifth D.A.C. had been ordered to move to Fremont at 4 a.m. and there await further orders. At Fremont it would be equally well placed either to retire or to supply ammunition if necessary.

At dawn (4 a.m.) R.F.A. Brigade commanders and the B.C. of 108

---

1. Acting with the 13th Inf. Bde., thus replacing XV. R.F.A. & 14th Inf. Bde. who had performed that duty on Aug. 25th.
2. On the night 25/26, 2/Suffolk R. & 2/Manchester R. (14th Inf. Bde.) had bivouacked at & near Pont des Quatre Vaux whilst the rest of the 14th Inf. Bde., 1/D.C.L.J. & 1/E. Surrey R. (less 2 coys.), with 14th B.H.Q. lay to the E. of Le Cateau itself. On falling in at dawn all these units were under the impression that the retreat would be continued on Aug. 26. Second Corps Operation Order No. 6, issued at 10.15 p.m. Aug. 25, ordered the main bodies to start at 7 a.m. on Aug. 26.

Heavy Battery met the C.R.A., as arranged overnight, to carry out the reconnaissance of the position; but as a retirement had now been ordered this precaution became unnecessary, when the counter-order was received some golden minutes had been wasted. Further, the Fifth Divisional front was now to extend from the high ground beyond Le Cateau to Troisvilles (inclusive) so any detailed reconnaissance became out of the question. As the front was between four and five miles in length this precluded any central supervision of the divisional artillery, also it was practically impossible for the brigade of howitzers to control the German guns from any central position.

Consequently the C.R.A. detailed a brigade of 18-pdrs. to each section of the line allotted to the three infantry brigades of the division, attached a howitzer battery to each of the flank brigades, and ordered their commanders to come into action at once in close co-operation with the infantry defence.[3] Thus XV R.F.A., with 37 (Hows.) of VIII R.F.A., were to co-operate with the 14th Infantry Brigade holding the right section on the east of the Roman Road; XXVIII R.F.A., as already arranged, would act with the 13th Infantry Brigade in the centre section, holding the big spur to the west of the Roman Road; whilst XXVII R.F.A. (less 120), with 65 (Hows.), were detailed to work with the 15th Infantry Brigade holding the left section, from the big spur just mentioned to Troisvilles (inclusive).

At 4 a.m. orders had been sent to XV R.F.A. to move towards Le Cateau; naturally these orders contained no indication that an action was to be fought, as the decision to stand and fight had not yet reached the C.R.A. On receipt of the orders the brigade moved forward and then halted in the valley, in mass, midway between Reumont and the Pont des Quatre Vaux.

Lieut.-Col. Stevens, commanding XV R.F.A., at once went forward towards the Pont des Quatre Vaux to confer with the B.G.C. 14th Infantry Brigade. Meanwhile XXVIII R.F.A. had already reached its allotted ground; and the C.O. of XXVII R.F.A., on hearing of the change of plan, proceeded immediately to the front to report to the infantry brigadier under whom he was to work.

Thus, despite the unfavourable weather of the previous evening and the unavoidable loss of time through changes in plan, very prompt arrangements were made in the Fifth Division for the co-operation of

3. The arrangement of attaching a howitzer battery to a brigade of 18-pdrs., so early in the war, is especially interesting in view of the permanent alteration in the organisation of the field artillery that occurred later on.

its artillery with the infantry allotted to hold the very exposed flank of the line.

As the action was obviously a delaying one naturally the C.R.A. kept in hand only the smallest proportion of his command. At first this reserve of artillery consisted of one 18-pr. Battery (120 of XXVII), one 4.5" Howitzer Battery (61 of VIII) and the 108 Heavy Battery.

The general idea that was to underlie the employment of the artillery in this division on August 26 was that the howitzers and 60-pdrs. should be used primarily for counter-battery work, whilst the 18-pdrs. would co-operate closely with their infantry in resisting to the last every German attack. The idea of holding on at all costs was very marked throughout this division.

Note.—The diaries furnish evidence that it is very hard to reconcile; but this is not uncommon, and it is often due to the exaggerated brevity of the diary.

The C.R.A. in his account states that during the night 25/26, orders had been received to continue the retirement, and implies that the counter-order, to stand and fight it out, did not reach him till after 4 a.m. on August 26, when the officers had assembled for the reconnaissance. This is borne out by the action of XXVIII which moved about 3 a.m. to take up a rearguard position.

O.C. XXVII states, however, that at 1.30 p.m. (a.m.?) he received orders from the C.R.A. grouping his brigade temporarily with the 15th Infantry Brigade. He started immediately on foot to report to the B.G.C. in question.

The diary of the 108 H.B. states that, at 12.30 a.m., orders were received that the Le Cateau position was to be held, 108 H.B. forming part of the artillery reserve under the C.R.A., and adds that the reconnaissance took place at 4.30 a.m. on August 26. It must not be overlooked that the corps conference at Bertry was not held until about 2 a.m. (*Vide* start chapter 5.)

In the foregoing description the C.R.A's account has been followed.

(b) Third Division—(See map 3.)

In the diaries available for this divisional artillery the changes of plan are not apparent.[4] It appears certain that the brigade ammunition

---

4. It has been ascertained that on 20 Aug. XLII. R.F.A. (41 not having yet rejoined) was detailed as part of the rearguard to the Third Division. (Continued next page).

columns commenced retiring but receiving counter-orders, on the march, they turned northward to the battlefield which they reached in ample time. The only evidence available refers to the XL B.A.C. This column had bivouacked to the east of Caudry overnight; it paraded at dawn and then moved off to the south past Clary towards Elincourt.[5]

The section of the battlefield allotted to the Third Division (7th, 8th, and 9th Infantry Brigades) ran from Troisvilles (exclusive) through Audencourt to Caudry (inclusive) and the fighting troops were available on the spot for they had bivouacked on this line.

About 3.30 a.m. the batteries of XXIII R.F.A. took up a position of readiness behind the Audencourt ridge, about three-quarters of a mile west of Troisvilles.

In order to occupy the forward positions unobserved, the section of 108 (Lt. E. L. B. Anderson) moved forward at 3.30 a.m. and occupied their pits before the light came. 108 rounds per gun were provided—a very suitable number. The detachments at once set to work to improve the positions which were about 300 yards in front of the crest and rather more than that distance behind the left battalion (1 /Lincolnshire Regiment) of the 9th Infantry Brigade.

At 4.30 a.m. XXIII R.F.A. came into action behind the ridge, having two sections in action in pits on the forward slope, to rake the approaches from Inchy and give close support to the 9th Infantry Brigade (forming the right of the Third Division) when the German attack was pressed home.[6]

These are all the movements that can be traced in this divisional artillery at dawn on Wednesday; but they were quite sufficient to ensure immediate support for the infantry should an attack develop as

These troops were to be in position at 7 a.m. It must be remembered that XLII., XXX (Hows.)) and the 7th Infantry Brigade only reached Caudry late on the previous night, the infantry being very exhausted.

5. The S.A.A. Carts of the XL. B.A.C. went straight to Audencourt and remained in that village. They were blown up there when the place was bombarded and set on fire during the action.

6. The sections were the centre of 107 and right of 108. In this connection it is interesting to note that for the defence of the outpost position held by the Third Division on the Mons Canal, on 23rd Aug., the C.R.A. of the Third Division had also employed advanced sections—1 section 49 R.F.A. on Hill 62, N.E. of Mons, 2 sections of 109 R.F.A. behind a barricade across two streets on the southern outskirts of Mons, and 2 sections of 107 and 108 R.F.A. entrenched to the S. of the town on Mt. Erebus. At Le Cateau Lt.-Col. A. T. Butler, commanding XXIII R.F.A., applied the same idea.

the light broke and the heavy mist rolled away.[7]

(c) Fourth Division.

No arrangements or movements are traceable among this divisional artillery at dawn August 26. Until 5.30 a.m. the mist appears to have been very thick; but, as the order to occupy the position was not issued until 6 a.m. in this division, (see note following), and no artillery diary mentions the low visibility, it is possible that the light had improved before any of the batteries unlimbered.

> Note:—Fourth Division Operation Order No. 1, issued at 5 p.m. on Aug. 25 from Viesly, contained the following paragraphs:—
>
> > 1. First and Second Corps are taking up a position on the line Avesnes—Le Cateau—Caudry (inclusive), the Third Division on the left.
> > 2. The Fourth Division will take up a position Caudry (exclusive)—Fontaine au pire—Wambaix—Knoll just north of Serainviller, and will commence entrenching as soon as it is light tomorrow . . . .
>
> This order was written when the first plan was issued to the B.E.F., that the intention was to offer battle on the Le Cateau line. Apparently it was never countermanded in the Fourth Division. The opening paragraph of the Divisional Operation Order, issued at 6 a.m. on Aug. 26 (given in Appendix 1) distinctly alludes to it.

(d) Royal Horse Artillery.[8]

III R.H.A.

"D" R.H.A. paraded at 4 a.m. and commenced to move back towards Bazuel.

In VII R.H.A., "L" (and "E") also moved at 1 a.m. to some unspecified place on the right flank.[9]

"I" stood to at dawn. The B.C., being out of touch with his cavalry brigade, went to the brigade commander of XLII for instructions.[10] It was suggested that "I" should join XLII temporarily, to replace 41.

---

7. It will be more convenient to consider the ground in this section when the whole of the divisional artillery are deployed.

8. The records are very scanty.

9. The first movements of "L" R.H.A. appear to indicate a continuation of the retirement. The counter-order possibly reached the battery at Maurois.

10. "I" had marched from Viesly to Caudry with XLII.

Major Thompson fell in with this suggestion and returned to "I" so as to have the battery ready to join XLII when the rearguard was formed at 7 a.m. Having turned up the street leading to the west face of Caudry, where the battery had halted overnight, the B.C. was met by rifle bullets whistling down the street. At about the same time firing—gun and rifle—broke out to the north of Caudry. The pursuing German Army had established contact.

CHAPTER 7

Deployment of the Artillery—
5 to 6 a.m.

(a) Fifth Division. (See Map 2 and Sketch B.).

It will be recollected that in this division there were four main
groups of artillery—on the Right, XV, with 37 (Hows.) attached; in
the Centre, XXVIII; on the Left, XXVII (less 120), with 65 (Hows.)
attached; and in Reserve, behind the Centre, 120 of XXVII, 61
(Hows.), and 108 Heavy Battery. It will be convenient to deal with
them in this order.

It was about 5 a.m.[1] when Lieut.-Colonel Stevens (Commanding
XV R.F.A.) met the C.R.A., Fifth Division, and received orders to
occupy the position which the brigade eventually took up.[2] A little
later the B.G.C. 14th Infantry Brigade informed Lieut.-Colonel Stevens that orders had been issued for the position to be held until 7.30
a.m. The brigade commander now ordered his batteries to come into
action as quickly as possible.

The B.C. of 52 R.F.A. unlimbered in a position he had selected
behind a small knoll in the valley about one and a quarter miles to
the north of Reumont (see Map 2 and Sketch B). About the same
time the B.C.'s of 11 and 80 R.F.A. rode forward to receive their
orders from their brigade commander. It was at this moment, probably between 5.30 and 5.45 a.m., that Lieut.-Colonel Stevens received
definite news, from an A.D.C. of the Fifth Division, that the Second
Corps was to stand and fight on its present position.

1. Until the action opens the times given by Lieut.-Col. Stevens have been followed
for XV. R.F.A.
2. A short time before these orders were issued the C.R.A. pointed out to the B.C.
of 37 (Hows.) the position his battery was to occupy. It was taken up at once.

Immediately afterwards the B.G.C. 14th Infantry Brigade informed him that there would be no retirement.[3] The positions selected for the two right batteries of the brigade were pointed out on the ground. That allotted to 11, suitably on the right of the fine, was very exposed. But the brigade commander stated that the First Corps was going to co-operate in the action and would occupy the high ground to the east of the Selle valley and thus cover the open flank of 11, which would otherwise have been exposed to a destructive enfilade fire from that ridge.

XV (less 52 R.F.A.) then moved forward and joined 37 (Hows.), taking up a position in the open which they entrenched as thoroughly as possible. The brigade commander also ordered 52 to move forward and come into action on the left of the rest of the brigade. By the time the battery had unlimbered, in the new position, 37 had almost finished digging in. To assist the guns in resisting to the last, in their forward position, in some cases (37 Hows, and 52) both wagons were brought up and placed alongside them. 11 and 80 had zones allotted to them by the brigade commander, whilst tasks were assigned to 37 (Hows.) and to 52.

Actually the B.C. of 11 had unlimbered his battery in a covered position about a quarter of a mile behind the one originally pointed out (see Map 2 and Sketch B); however, he received orders to move forward and the battery then came into action in the position that had been detailed in the first instance.

As his brigade had to co-operate closely with the 14th Infantry Brigade in a fight to a finish, Lieut.-Colonel Stevens considered that all his batteries must unlimber in the forward position originally indicated by the C.R.A.; consequently he ordered forward 11 and 52. Owing to this advance to the forward position 11, like 52, was left with very little time to dig in and practically all that could be done before the action was to "*camouflage*" the guns by fastening some of the corn-stooks on the gun-shields.

As the battery was now placed, the right of the main position of the 2/Suffolk Regiment was immediately in front of its right gun, whilst the battery was liable to be enfiladed by any guns unlimbering on or behind the ridge south of Le Cateau as well as by any German batteries in action near Neuvilly. Le Cateau might be as glorious a war service for 11 as Minden, but the battery would be fortunate if it was

---

3. It is quite dear from the available evidence that the subordinate commanders on this flank had no idea that only a delaying action was contemplated.

able to leave its mark on the Germans before it was silenced. [4]

So immediately to the left of 11 was better placed, for a slight swell between the two batteries defiladed 80 from the ridge beyond the Selle, whilst the battery was also sheltered in front from machine-gun fire. Unfortunately this last mentioned cover made it almost impossible for 80 to deal with its own allotted zone.

About 100 yards further to the left were 37 (Hows.) astride a country road. This battery obtained a certain amount of natural cover; also, being first on the ground, the men had more time for entrenchment and in the reaped cornfield digging was fairly easy.

Immediately beyond the howitzers 52 had unlimbered m the open. The guns were in a small depression in a root-field, but this hollow was insufficient to give either full cover or concealment and the rising ground behind the battery made it difficult to get at the guns from the rear. 52 was bound to suffer very heavily in this position, once it was located and seriously engaged. A further disadvantage was that the right section could only clear the crest at 1400 yards. To the northward, however, a good distant view was obtainable, only limited by a ridge about 5000 yards off. To ensure for the battery a certain supply of ammunition both wagons were brought up for each gun and placed alongside it.

The Battery O.P. was about 200 yards in front of the guns and was on the forward slope, in line with the trenches of the 2/Suffolk Regiment. From the O.P. the gun-flashes alone were visible and a telephone was laid out to connect the B.C. with his battery.

Whilst 52 was preparing for action Lieut.-Colonel Stevens issued orders to the B.C. that "we would fight it out here and there would be no retirement." Major Nutt then went down into the battery and explained this order to all ranks. Before 6 a.m. the battery was ready for action. A hostile aeroplane now flew over the brigade and subsequent events prove that it located the batteries.

The O.P. for XV and 37 was placed in the only possible situation

---

4. 11 R.F.A., formerly A/XI., was Captain Forbes Macbean's Heavy Brigade at Minden in 1759; its armament then was 10 12-pdrs. each drawn by 7 horses. During the battle it overpowered a French battery of 30 pieces. Through an error Captain Forbes Macbean was omitted from a mention in Prince Ferdinand's General Order. On discovering the oversight the prince wrote a letter in his own hand to Captain Forbes Macbean acknowledging his indebtedness to him and to his brigade. Captain Forbes Macbean was one of the witnesses at the Trial of Lord George Sackville. (Duncan's, *History of the R.A. I.* and *Trial of Lord George Sackville in 1760*. The two other Minden Batteries were descendants of the old *Train of Artillery* and they became 46 Coy., R.G.A. & 53 Coy. R.G.A. (reduced 1907).

on the tip of a small rise in front, from which a good view was obtainable and communication to the batteries was easy, although 37 was actually out of sight.[5] The B.C. of 80 observed in the open close to his guns. Thus the four batteries had come into action immediately behind the infantry line and actually in front of the troops who were in support in this section. Before the batteries were thoroughly dug in rifle-fire broke out.

Doubtless this exposed position was the best that could be selected, giving due consideration to the bad weather and poor visibility overnight, the counter-orders that were received, the shortness of time available for reconnaissance in the morning, and the early hour at which the action opened. Undoubtedly the readiness shown by the whole of the brigade to share the same risks as the 2/Suffolk Regiment, and the willingness of the batteries to take up a very exposed position in order to afford the closest support to their own infantry, had a great moral effect on the latter. Occurring at the commencement of the war this exhibition of real comradeship in a critical hour was bound to have a far reaching effect.

In the centre, XXVIII at dawn proceeded to the front to occupy a rearguard position. The brigade halted half-way down the forward slope whilst the ground was reconnoitred. The task was by no means easy, for the mist limited the view to the poplars along the Le Cateau[6]—Cambrai Road. The position finally selected by 122 was the best placed of the three,[7] and about 5 a.m. the battery unlimbered behind a low knoll that save cover from view but not flash cover.[8] Slight as it was it sufficed. The battery was never located and until the last phase hardly suffered at all.[9] 122 proceeded to dig itself in. 123

---

5. Communication between the O.P. and 37 was at first by telephone; after that cut flags were used. A telephone was used to connect the Brigade O.P. with 11 and 80. The O.P. for 52 was about 10 yards in front of the Bde O.P.

6. In several diaries and accounts, as well as in two sketches, it is quite clear that several officers confused Montay & Le Cateau, and the latter name is given by them to the small village. On Aug. 25 none of the artillery of the division had retired through Le Cateau itself. The only batteries to pass through the town on Aug. 25 were "D", "E" and "L" R.H.A. and 41 R.F.A. of the Third Divisional Artillery.

7. Apparently it was discovered by one of the battery officers.

8. It was about this time that the brigade learned the retirement was cancelled and the Second Corps was to hold the position, until the arrival of heavy reinforcements rendered possible a great counter attack.

9. The only casualties that occurred in 122, before the arrival of the limbers, were two successive layers of No. 1 gun, shot through the head by a sniper from the commanding 150-metre knoll to the right front of the battery.

entrenched in a cornfield in the open, about 200 yards to the north-west of 122. These two batteries were in action only a short distance behind the firing line itself.

Although 123 had a few infantry in front of it, yet its only screen was the trees along the Cambrai road, consequently these positions did not err on the side of over-caution. 124 came into action about 100 yards in rear of 123 with a zone of fire to the west, the idea being that it should flank the front of the 13th Infantry Brigade. Owing to the mist and the uncertain positions occupied by these troops it was very difficult to allot the zone accurately at that early hour. (Apparently the battery never fired in this direction.) Being just behind 123 and at right angles to it, 124 was very liable to be raked by any shell that ranged beyond the former. On taking up their positions these three batteries at once dug in.[10]

The O.P. of XXVIII was in the short length of cutting (three feet to four feet deep) immediately in rear of the brigade and close to the headquarters of the 13th Infantry Brigade. At the opening of the action 123's O.P. was also in the same cutting.[11]

Thus the right and centre R.F.A. Brigades of the Fifth Division had taken the injunction "to co-operate closely with its infantry" in the most literal sense. Nearly all the battery positions were exposed to view and also to enfilade fire, and coming into action as they did on the forward slope there could hardly be any retirement. But quite undaunted by the outlook the batteries proceeded to make every preparation for a fight to a finish.

At 5.30 a.m., the following message was sent from the Fifth Divisional Headquarters to the 13th Infantry Brigade:—

Operation Order No. 4 is modified, in that the fighting troops will hold their positions.

Immediately to the west the ground was more suitable and different dispositions were made in XXVII which was co-operating with the 15th Infantry Brigade.

119 was brought into action behind the ridge about 1,500 yards to the east of Troisvilles with its O.P. in the road to the north-east of

---

10. Whilst digging in 123 came under rifle-fire from some Germans working up the valley from Montay.
11. The sunken road, in which the O.P.'s. were placed, had several short lengths of cutting where it crossed the small ridges on the back of the spur across which it ran to Troisvilles.

that village.[12] 121 unlimbered in a valley-head immediately to the east of Troisvilles with an O.P. close at hand. The Brigade O.P. of XXVII was in a hollow road close to the *Arbre* and alongside the B.G.C., 15th Infantry Brigade.

The Howitzer Battery allotted to this section—65—had come into action at an early hour to the south-west of Troisvilles.[13] It was well concealed and adequately entrenched, it was practically never located.

With reference to the Reserve, 61 (Hows.) came into action under cover in rear of the left centre of the Fifth Division. Its position was about 1,500 yards to the north of Reumont and to the west of the Roman Road. Before the action opened the battery had dug itself in. 108 Heavy Battery unlimbered behind the spur that runs north from Reumont, having its O.P. on the rising ground to the front. These two batteries were admirably placed, both to take an effective hand in the action as well as to cover the retirement of the Fifth Division when the Second Corps had completed its task.

120 of XXVII was never used in the Fifth Division; it was lent to the Third Division during the morning and then came into action near the *Arbre* to support the 9th Infantry Brigade.

The C.R.A., Fifth Division, had his headquarters at Reumont, which was also the divisional headquarters.[14]

(b) Third Division—(See Map .3).

In this division XLII R.F.A. was allotted to the 7th Infantry Brigade, whilst the rest of the divisional artillery was kept directly under the control of the C.R.A.

It will be recollected that both XXIII [15] and XL had unlimbered about dawn. When the German guns opened on Caudry from the north the previous rearguard orders were clearly cancelled. Consequently the two batteries of XLII at once moved forward and unlim-

---

12. This identification of the O.P. of 119 is from the brigade diary. The position selected for the battery (119) turned out to be rather an unfortunate fine. The guns could only fire at long ranges, owing to the difficulty of clearing the crest of the hill.

13. See Map 3.

14. The authorities for placing the various batteries on Map 2 are as follows:—For XV, 37 (Hows.), XXVIII, 61 (Hows.), and 108 Heavy Battery, officers of various units present at Le Cateau. For XXVII & 65 (Hows.), sketch by C.R.A., Fifth Division, attached to his diary.

15. The mist was thick until about 6 a.m. when it cleared off. The forward section of 108 had used the extra hour for work on its pits. When they got the first view towards Inchy it was satisfactory to find that the necessary ground was well covered.

bered on the *chaussée* to the north-east of the town.[16] This action was the one best suited to meet the critical situation that had arisen.

XXX (Hows.) R.F.A. had reached Caudry at midnight; at 3 a.m. they came into action to the south-west of that place. Thus the bulk of the town screened them on the north side, whilst they were covered in front by the ridge just to the west of Caudry. But the brigade never fired from this position and at 8 a.m. it moved back to a covered position in the Warnelle Ravine.

Towards 6 a.m. 48 Heavy Battery also came into action about 300 yards behind the Audencourt ridge, to the south-south-east of that village, and dug in there, with its O.P. close at hand to prevent the use of a long telephone line. The country was too wet to allow the battery to occupy a position further back in the fields.

The Third D.A.C., directly it was certain that an action was to be fought, arranged for the re-supply of ammunition. In advance were placed the Heavy and Howitzer section at Bertry and another section at Clary; the two remaining sections were at Elincourt and Malincourt, with the headquarters of the column to the north of Maretz.

Although in this section of the front held by the Third Division there was a distinct salient—the large village of Caudry—yet the general position was easier to occupy than that of the Fifth Division on the right. The Third Division held the centre of the line, and the ground itself was more favourable for defence. Instead of three large spurs jutting towards the enemy, with a covered line of approach immediately outside its right flank—up the valley of the Selle through the town of Le Cateau—as was the case in the section allotted to the Fifth Division, the ground held by the Third Division mainly consisted of a long ridge that ran athwart the line of advance from the north.

This ridge provided not only suitably covered positions for the batteries, but the valley in rear of it—the Warnelle Ravine—could be used as a shielded way from flank to flank. The only serious defects were the two villages of Audencourt and Caudry, for there was no time to prepare them properly for defence, although the infantry were bound to hold them to prevent the Germans from gaining an immediate and vital lodgement on the ridge. Except for this disadvantage, this part of the position if appropriately prepared was quite strong enough to offer a serious battle on.

In this area, having no flanks to guard and a shorter length to

---

16. It was arranged that "I" should come into action alongside XLII, but no suitable position could be found.

defend, the C.R.A. deployed the whole force of artillery, and the disposition of XXIII R.F.A., with its two sections dug in on the forward slope, was admirable. The headquarters of the C.R.A., Third Division, were close to 48 Heavy Battery, whilst the Third Division's headquarters were at Bertry. During the action an advanced headquarters was formed close to 48 Heavy Battery.[17]

(c) Fourth Division—(See Maps 4 and 5.).

In this division, which had only reached its billets after dark on the previous night, an Operation Order was issued at 6 a.m. for the division to take up a defensive line from Le Coquelet Farm to Moulin d'Esnes.[18] The 11th Infantry Brigade was to hold the right and the 12th Infantry Brigade the left of the allotted space, being separated by the railway to the south of Fontaine-au-pire. This left in reserve the 10th Infantry Brigade, a very necessary precaution as this was quite obviously the vital flank; and the French cavalry corps, under General Sordet, which had reached their position to the west on the previous night, was an independent force.

At 6.15 a.m. the C.R.A. issued the orders to his brigades. XXXII R.F.A. and XXXVII (Hows.) R.F.A. were to reconnoitre suitable positions to the east of the d'Iris Stream, whilst XIV and XXIX R.F.A. did so to the west. Meanwhile, to be ready as soon as they were wanted, XIV and XXIX R.F.A. were to take up positions of readiness to the south-east of Esnes, taking the necessary pre- cautious to cover their open left flank. [19]

Brigade ammunition columns were to establish themselves to the south of the positions selected for their own brigades.

In this division it is clear that nothing could be done overnight, because the troops were employed in covering the last stage of the retirement of the Third Division. Directly it became certain in the morning that the Second Corps was to stand and fight, everything that was possible was done to distribute the batteries in the way most suitable for immediate co-operation with the infantry defence.

The position was difficult because the left flank was in the air and distinctly threatened. The Germans had apparently occupied Cam-

---

17. The principal authority for placing the batteries in Map 3 is a sketch accompanying the diary of the C.R.A., Third Division. Wherever possible reference has been made to officers who were present at the action for verification and, further details.
18. A copy is given in Appendix 1.
19. XXIX R.F.A. apparently started for Esnes at 6 a.m. It must be recollected that all the artillery of this division halted at Ligny on the previous night.

brai the previous night. Further, the long spur running to the north of the Warnelle Ravine provided cover for the German guns which could never be accurately located once the ridge of the spur passed definitely into German hands. [20] Also the ground to the south of the Warnelle Ravine was largely a series of spurs running north towards the assailants; suitable covered positions would therefore be difficult to find close behind the infantry, particularly when the Germans had crowned the ridge and established their O.P.'s on it.

The absence of the Heavy Battery was certain to be felt by the infantry, particularly in the early stages of the engagement. [21]

The headquarters of the C.R.A., Fourth Division, were at Hau-court, and divisional headquarters were also in this village at the commencement of the action. About noon D.H.Q. were moved to the south-west of Caullery.[22]

(d) Royal Horse Artillery.

The first movements of "D", "E", and "L" have already been mentioned.

"I" R.H.A.

When the firing broke out around the north end of Caudry, Major Thompson at once went back to XLII to arrange for "I" to co-operate with the two field batteries in the most effective way. Finding no suitable position for "I" on the *chaussée* to the left of XLII the battery commander finally discovered positions for two isolated guns on the north-western edge of Caudry. These were occupied at once. From these positions German infantry could be seen among the corn-stooks to the left front. The guns had unlimbered in the nick of time.

---

20. At that time no aeroplane communication and co-operation with the field batteries was attempted.

21. Probably this fact accounts for the numerous statements that have been made to the effect that the division was without its artillery until the afternoon of Aug. 26.

22. Practically the only authority for placing the batteries in Map 4 is a sketch made by the B.M.R.A., Fourth Division, forming part of the appendices of the G.S. Diary of the Fourth Division for August 1914. The sketch does not entirely agree with the diaries. As far as possible the sketch has been followed, because the differences may be accounted for by the rather vague way in which some of the positions are described in the diaries.

CHAPTER 8

The Action of Le Cateau
(Continued)

(A.). THE OPENING OF THE ACTION. 6—9 A.M.
(See Maps 2 and 5, and Sketch B.

At the outset the 19th Infantry Brigade, which had bivouacked overnight near Le Cateau Railway Station, passed through the town and marched past the Pont des Quatre Vaux in order to reach its place in the retiring column.[1] The head of the brigade debouched from Le Cateau at 5.30 a.m., but before the column was clear of the town its rearguard collided in the streets with Germans.

To the east of Le Cateau, at 6.30 a.m., as the detached portion of the 14th Infantry Brigade[2] was about to commence its march through the town in order to concentrate with the rest of its brigade and take its place in the marching column, a heavy rifle fire was opened on it from the eastern end of Le Cateau and soon after it came under shell fire. Rallying immediately from the first surprise the two regiments made a fine fighting retirement along the spur to the south, in which General Gough's cavalry and "D" Battery, R.H.A., co-operated. The spur of Le Cateau was clear of our infantry by noon.[3]

This unfortunate occurrence laid bare, from the start of the Action, the right flank of the troops of the Fifth Division west of Le Cateau, who were holding the spur to the east of the Roman Road. The units immediately affected being the 2/Suffolk Regiment and XV R.F.A.

---

1. The counter-orders did not reach the troops south and east of Le Cateau.
2. Brigade Signal Section and 1 East Surrey Regt. (less 2 cos.) & 1/D.C.L.I.; the last-named was to lead the column.
3. In their advance against this portion of the 14th Infantry Brigade it was noticed that the Germans came on extended, at about 5 paces interval.

with 37 (Hows.), all of whom had received orders to maintain their positions to the last. From the very outset therefore the Germans possessed a covered line of approach—the valley of the Selle—and a covered concentration area—Le Cateau itself. The situation on the right was critical from the commencement.

(a) Fifth Division. (See Map 2).

It was soon after 6 a.m. that the German artillery opened fire[4] from the direction of Neuvilly. XV R.F.A. and 37 (Hows.) replied at once, they engaged gun-flashes at a range of about 5000 yards and silenced two of the hostile batteries. But the Germans bringing more batteries into action subjected the brigade to a very heavy and accurate fire, chiefly high-explosive with an occasional burst of shrapnel, causing many casualties in the gun detachments. [5] As our own batteries had been ordered not to fire too freely at first most of the ammunition was saved for use against the German infantry when they should deliver their assault.

About 6.15 a.m. German infantry were seen from the O.P. of 52 advancing m columns over the crest of the ridge to the northward and about 5000 yards away. This was a chance to be seized at once and the Battery immediately opened on the target. The fire caused the German infantry to deploy, but pressing on down the slope they soon disappeared from view.

Shortly before 7 a.m. one salvo of H.E. burst over the XV Brigade O.P., killing a bombardier and wounding both Lieut.-Colonel Stevens and Major Jones, commanding 37 (Hows.). Captain Leech (adjutant), Lieut. Younger (orderly officer) and the battery-sergeant-major of 37 (Hows.) were struck by shell-fragments. All remained at their posts.

2nd Lieut. E. H. Broadhurst, commanding the centre section of 52, was severely wounded about this time and rendered incapable of carrying on. He refused to allow himself to be removed from the battery.

Against XXVIII the fire opened from the north-east, from the direction of Forest, probably a little later than in the case of XV. 122 was never found; but 123 was subjected to the converging fire of three batteries, one in front and one on each flank. The telephone wire being cut the B.C. came down to the battery. Shortly afterwards

---

4. The time given varies considerably; the B.C. of 52 states it was about 6.10 a.m.

5. The 2/Suffolk R. also suffered very heavily from this fire directed against our batteries; being hastily entrenched, only at a short distance in front of XV, most of the shell that burst short of the guns took effect on the infantry.

the Germans got a direct hit on No. 2 gun which put the gun and detachment out of action, and wounded the section commander and the B.C.; Captain A. G. Gillman thereupon assumed the command.

124 had undergone a very trying experience. When the fire first opened from the north-east the battery, entrenched facing northwest, was unable to reply. The fire also took the battery in reverse. The only way to obtain shelter was for the detachments to move round and crouch under the fronts of the gun-shields. Not long afterwards the original position of 124 became really untenable, for all the overs fired at 123 by the battery in front burst in 124, raking it from end to end. Consequently Major Kinsman and his battery manhandled the four right guns round in order to engage the German artillery. As a result of this manoeuvre Major Kinsman's right section were now about 100 yards in rear of 123 and fired directly over that battery. For the rest of the action these four guns were fought in the open.

A sketch will make this change clear:—

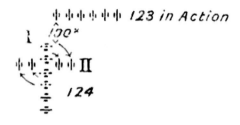

For this sketch I am indebted to the battery commander.

In XXVII both 119 and 121 responded promptly and adequately to the opening bombardment by the German guns, and concealment being far easier in this part of the field the Germans failed to locate the batteries which did not suffer at all heavily. Towards 8 a.m. 65 (Hows.) located one of a pair of German batteries that were shelling this area and, turning on to it at 3,500 yards, silenced it.

With the Reserve, 61 (Hows.) opened first on German guns to the north, but the observation was very difficult owing to trees.

108 Heavy Battery also strengthened the response to the German artillery, and fired away steadily, searching likely localities. Little more could be done at first, for the misty morning made it impossible to locate their batteries accurately.

Thus at the outset the conditions were very much in the German favour. They could select covered positions on a wide arc for their very numerous batteries; a certain number of easy targets at moderate ranges were presented to them whilst the light was still defective; the high-explosive shell carried in their field equipment gave them an undeniable advantage in counter-battery work, and the spire of Le Cateau Church furnished them with a magnificent O.P. overlooking the right flank of our position.

(b) Third Division—(See Map 3)

Although the C.R.A. had been linked up by telephone with XXIII as well as with his brigade of howitzers and his Heavy Battery, yet early in the fight the wires were all cut by shells and thereafter mounted orderlies had to be employed. In this part of the front great difficulty was experienced in locating the German batteries with real accuracy. This difficulty was mutual, for here the enemy could obtain no flank O.P's to assist him in controlling his fire, and the back of the well marked ridge, on which stands the village of Audencourt, provided numerous covered positions for guns.

About 6.30 a.m., XXIII was lucky enough to get some infantry targets moving down the far slope, in order to establish a firing line along a sunken road running from Beaumont to the north end of Caudry. In this way an advance of German infantry from the direction of Bethencourt, against the 7th Infantry Brigade, was enfiladed by 109 and a section of 107. A little later a warm reception was accorded by 107 and a section of 108 to more infantry advancing over the rolling ground north of Inchy against the 7th Infantry Brigade. The good effect produced at this early stage, by the well placed batteries of XXIII R.F.A., was not forgotten later in the day when attempts were made by the German infantry to advance against our centre.

North of Caudry the situation was critical at the outset. But the two batteries of XLII gradually gained the mastery over the German guns and this early attack was beaten off. The exposed position on the Cambrai *chaussée*, however, could not be maintained indefinitely.[6]

Probably about 8 a.m.[7] XLII was ordered back to a position on the high ground near Tronquoy. It moved off in this direction, leaving a section of 29 near Caudry as a temporary measure.

It was about 8 a.m. when XXX (Hows.) also moved back to their

---

6. XLII was in action in front of the position selected for the infantry firing line.
7. The time is uncertain. The brigade diary says "about 9 a.m." this would appear to be rather late. The B.C. of "I" R.H.A. is inclined to place it as early as 7 a.m. A mean has been struck provisionally.

second position in the valley just north of the railway. The artillery of the division was now echeloned in depth; and, when the time came to retire, batteries were well placed to cover the withdrawal from the firing line.

Meanwhile 48 Heavy Battery had been employed in counter-battery work, but the well-concealed German batteries were extremely difficult to locate. Happily their return fire was for a time ineffective. After a German aeroplane had flown over the 60-pdrs., the shelling became more accurate, but even then the Heavy Battery was never properly located and hardly suffered any casualties.

41 R.F.A. (of XLII), having formed part of the rear party on August 25,[8] was marching all through the night with the 2/Royal Irish Rifles, with which it had been co-operating. Moving through Montay, Le Cateau,[9] Pont des Quatre Vaux,[10] and Reumont, (see Map 5), the column halted in the early morning at Maurois, and awaited further orders; here the horses were watered and fed, and the men got a much appreciated breakfast.[11] Whilst in this position the action commenced and the battery stood to. Orders were now received from Second Corps H.Q. for the column to proceed to Bertry.[12] The battery moved on[13] and halted about half-a-mile to the east of Tronquoy, where the B.C. concealed it under the edge of a small copse to hide it from aeroplane observation whilst he reconnoitred. The action was in full swing, and our position was spread out in front of 41 like a great map.

Here in the centre it is quite clear that the Third Divisional Artillery suffered very little damage during the German bombardment and reserved itself to deal with the German infantry directly they showed themselves.

But the pressure on Caudry began to increase towards the end of this phase; and at 8.20 a.m. the Third Division reported to the Second Corps that Caudry was attacked on both flanks and asked for the co-operation of the Fourth Division.

---

8. The rear party lost touch of the rest of the rear guard of the Third Division before reaching Solesmes.
9. It took three hours to get through Le Cateau.
10. The wrong road was taken here for some distance.
11. Some .supply lorries were met at Reumont. and forage and food were drawn from them.
12. On passing through Bertry, General Sir H. Smith Dorrien was seen outside ibis H.Q. His confident bearing made a great impression on all ranks.
13. The 2 R. Irish Rifles took up a position near Tronquoy.

(c) Fourth Division—(See Maps 4 and 5).

In this section the 11th Infantry Brigade held the right of the line along the spur, north of the Warnelle Ravine, in front of Ligny; whilst the 12th Infantry Brigade held the left flank in front of Haucourt. The divisional artillery came into action as follows: XXXII were detailed to support 11th Infantry Brigade, and 27 unlimbered in the open to the west of the village of Ligny, whilst 134 took position, under cover, immediately to the south-west of that place, and 135 was behind cover to the left rear of 27, though it did not fire from this position.

The 11th Infantry Brigade had asked for artillery co-operation to divert from them some of the German gunfire to which they were being subjected. Consequently XXXII were brought into action as rapidly as possible. 27 came into action among the corn-stooks in a stubble-field, and about twenty-five yards in front of a hollow road, the O.P. being on the right, on slightly higher ground, about forty yards away.

XXIX were ordered into action south-east of Haucourt to co-operate with the 11th Infantry Brigade, north of the Warnelle Ravine. 127 to the south of the village fired mainly in the direction of the quarries in front of the 11th Infantry Brigade. 120 more to the south fired chiefly to the east of Moulin d'Esnes. 125 was on the right bank of the Iris Stream to the east of 126, and was used largely for counter-battery work along the ridge north of the ravine.

XXXVII (Hows.) came into action in the d'Iris valley facing north, but whilst in this position did not fire. XIV moved to Haucourt at 7 a.m. and on arrival found the infantry sharply engaged. Its duty was to support the 12th Infantry Brigade, and 68 came into action at once just west of the village, [14] 39 was about three-quarters of a mile in rear, with 88 in the valley-head to the east of S. Aubert Fme.

It was nearing 7 a.m. when the German onslaught opened seriously in this quarter. Then their vastly superior artillery and machine-guns prepared and covered an attack on Haucourt. [15] A vigorous artillery duel was the immediate result, and during its continuance there can be no doubt the Fourth Division felt acutely the absence of its Heavy Battery.

---

14. The positions shown on the map for most of the batteries of the Fourth Division are only provisional for no brigade or battery sketches are available. The indications are vague, and in several cases contradictory, this is especially the case with XIV.
15. Opposite Longsart the advancing Germans were extended at 10 to 15 yards between files. It is probable that this attack was made by dismounted cavalry and *Jägers*.

In XXXII, both 27 and 134 searched for guns behind the ridge near Fontaine-au-pire. 27 being in action in the open drew down on itself a heavy return fire from several batteries, which it did its best to keep employed in order to draw the fire off its own infantry. Locating one battery (at 3650 yards)[16] 27 silenced it except one gun, direct hits being reported on two of the others. This German battery had been engaged shelling our Infantry, but their switch on to 27 was very slow, and 27 was able to begin battery fire before the Germans had finished ranging. The issue of that duel was then no longer in doubt. 27 was then engaged by two or three German batteries, and it became impracticable to bring up any more ammunition to the guns, the detachments therefore were withdrawn under cover until the German infantry advanced. Up to this moment the casualties inflicted on the battery had been very few, for most of the H.E. shell burst on or beyond the sunken road.

On this part of the front the attack at this stage was not pressed so strongly as it was against the right flank nor do there seem to have been so many hostile batteries in action. The Germans not having enveloped the open flank at the commencement of the action were unable to bring as heavy and accurate fire to bear on it as they did on the right flank in the vicinity of the Roman Road.

> Note:—Our air-reports during this phase give the following interesting facts:—
>
> At 9 a.m. a French division (probably Territorial) was in bivouac, at Gouzeaucourt (to the S. of Cambrai). At the same hour French cavalry were seen moving westwards from Malincourt. At this time no Germans were seen west of Cambrai; but several small columns, each about 2 miles long, were noticed on the move to the eastward of that town. One was marching down the Roman Road and had reached Englefontaine, another was closing on Solesmes from the N.E., whilst a third was halted on the Cambrai—Solesmes road, being about 5 miles to the east of the former.
>
> Unfortunately the air-reports for August 26 that are available at present contain no information about the effect of our fire and give very little indication of the position of any German batteries that were active during the action. There are no aerial

---

16. The range to the German guns was checked from the fuse of a shell that landed in the battery.

photographs available.

(d) Royal Horse Artillery—(See Map 5).

III R.H.A.

Moving westwards from Catillon with General H. Gough's Cavalry, it was not long before "D""found itself on the right flank of a big fight."[17] Very shortly afterwards (before 8 a.m.) "D" came into action to the south-west of Bazuel and remained there for a considerable time.[18] Whilst in this position the battery got occasional small targets away to the north-east and north of Le Cateau, and gave some support to the l/D.C.L.L, whose retirement was closely pressed. But it is quite clear that the Germans made no determined attempt to work round this flank in force until much later in the action and this very exposed battery managed to maintain its advanced position and finally to withdraw without trouble.

Its presence, so wide on the right, no doubt assisted very materially the successful retirement of the 1/East Surrey Regiment, and the l/D. C.L.I, of the 14th Infantry Brigade who had been surprised at 6.30 a.m. to the east of Le Cateau.

"E" had moved with General Briggs and the I Cavalry Brigade, and having unlimbered in a covered position to the north of Escaufort the battery fired a few rounds whenever an opportunity arose.

VII R.H.A. "L" R.H.A., working with General Briggs' column, was responsible for covering the right flank of the Second Corps. "L" accordingly unlimbered in the valley to the east of Honnechy and north of Escaufort, but the information is only sufficient to place it in a conventional manner. The valley was clearly an uncomfortable position; it was bound to become untenable directly the German guns unlimbered on the S. Benin spur only about 2,500 yards to the eastward.

The two guns of "I" R.H.A., which had come into action on the outskirts of Caudry, opened on the German infantry in the cornfield to the northwest. After the guns had fired about 20 rounds each the surviving Germans retired hastily from close contact. The two guns remained in position until XLII was ordered to move south of the Warnelle Ravine, when "I" also withdrew to the high ground near Montigny. Its brief intervention at Caudry had been as valuable as it was timely.

---

17. The expression is to be found in the diary of "D" R.H.A.
18. Possibly as late as 1 p.m., but confirmation is required.

B. The Development of the Action. a.m. to noon.[19]
(a) Fifth Division—(See Map 2 and Sketch B).

At 9.25 a.m. an observer in an aeroplane saw a German brigade[20] unlimber on the high ground to the west of Forest, and immediately afterwards two more brigades[21] came into action on the same line. He could plainly see the British line to the south of the Cambrai road, its position being clearly marked by the German shells bursting all along it from the spur to the east of Pont des Quatre Vaux as far as Caudry. But he could locate no other German gun positions except those just to the west of Forest.

At 9.45 a.m. the Second Corps H.Q. at Bertry sent this message to the Fifth Division:—

> Do you think it is possible to spare one or two battalions to act as General Reserve at Bertry, as the situation is critical at Caudry.

The Fifth Division responded promptly to this request, and at 10.4 a.m. despatched the following answer

> Two battalions, 19th Infantry Brigade, are leaving for Bertry across country.

Following this up at 10.20 a.m. with another message,

> Am sending a battery of field guns[21] to Bertry as well as the two battalions, 19th Infantry Brigade.

This reinforcement for the centre reached Bertry about 11.30 a.m.,[22] and was then sent on to Montigny.

At 10.25 a.m. there were further indications that the action was going to take a serious turn on the right flank, for at this time the Fifth Division reported to corps headquarters that a German infantry column was moving down the Roman Road and that its head had already reached Montay.

---

19. At 11 a.m. General Joffre visited Field-Marshal Sir John French at the British G.H.Q. in S. Quentin and had a long interview. Early in the afternoon the commander-in-chief of the B.E.F. started to motor to the H.Q. of the IInd Corps. but he had to abandon the attempt as the roads were blocked with transport and refugees.—(commander-in-chief's diary).

20. Probably an *Abteilung*—18 guns—is meant in each case. In August 1914 a German brigade was 72 guns.

21. 126. of XXVII.

22. Its arrival was reported to the Fifth Division by a message timed 11.32 a.m.

By 10 a.m. the batteries of XV with 37 (Hows.) once more became active. The German infantry was now showing up and it was promptly subjected to a heavy and deadly fire, which commencing at 2,000 yards decreased steadily to 1,000 yards, and finally to 800 yards. For some time the German bombardment of these batteries was not so severe for XXVIII was drawing most of the fire, though it was during this period that 11 was shelled seriously for the first time. Two German guns opened on this battery from the big spur south of Le Cateau. At first the B.C. hesitated to answer this fire as he thought the First Corps were occupying the spur. Eventually he decided that a tree can only be judged by its fruit and as this was proving deadly in the extreme an immediate antidote was required.

Consequently the right section was refused and the section commander engaged the German guns. He succeeded in silencing them temporarily and almost immediately afterwards was wounded. The battery now began to suffer rather heavily from gun fire from the front as well as from the left flank, and as the action progressed German infantry were seen working up the Selle valley round the right flank. To meet this imminent danger the left section was run back (the gunners being assisted in their heavy task by some of the 2/Manchester Regiment) and the section commander engaged the German infantry at point-blank range. The reception accorded to the German infantry by these guns as well as the effect produced by the rifles and machine guns of the 2/Manchester Regiment, immediately on the right of the section, proved so disheartening to the assailants that for a time they discontinued further pressure in this dangerous quarter.

The casualties suffered by the personnel of 11 had been heavy, and at length the major, the only surviving officer, was wounded in the knee by a piece of shrapnel. However, he had the left gun of the refused right section swung round once more to the northward and remained in command of it, engaging any targets that appeared. This gun continued firing until about noon. The battery had amply sustained its old reputation.

The various positions of the guns of 11 are shown below.—

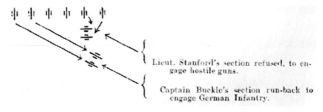

Lieut. Stanford's section refused, to engage hostile guns.

Captain Buckle's section run-back to engage German Infantry.

Immediately to the left of 11, 80 (although enfiladed from both flanks) kept in action and maintained a heavy and effective fire on any German infantry that showed, near Rambourlieux Farm, and drove them back. The corn-stooks behind which the Germans sought cover from the bursts of shrapnel proved a great disappointment. So fully employed was the battery that it expended the ammunition in its six wagons, whereupon three more were led up by the captain, two of which actually reached the guns. Major Birley also made every arrangement to push his guns up to the Suffolks' trenches should the Germans make any attempt to rush that battalion. Here on the exposed flank the artillery showed they realised fully that the greater the difficulties of their Infantry the closer and more intimate must be the support afforded by the guns.

37 (Hows.) during this phase of the action were also employed, at first, in shelling formed bodies of infantry. Later the battery turned on to advancing waves, covering a large area with its fire, until gradually it fired away nearly all the ammunition in both its wagon lines.

The left battery of the brigade, 52, was fought in the open under an extremely heavy fire. Before it had been definitely located 52 punished two German batteries severely. During the German bombardment a high-explosive burst over No. 5, knocked out the detachment and set the limber blankets ablaze. Not long afterwards a salvo of H.E. caught the battery and the centre section had to cease fire temporarily owing to damaged equipment and casualties. Nevertheless, the battery managed to fire all its available ammunition. Its captain then succeeded in reaching the guns with three more wagons, thus enabling the battery to continue shelling the German infantry who were now advancing to the east of Rambourlieux Farm.[23] It was suffering heavily itself from enfilade fire poured into it by German batteries to the north-west, and No. 4. had to cease firing on account of the danger to the Infantry in its front.

Shortly before noon German infantry were seen issuing from the wood to the north-west of Le Cateau and advancing towards the deep cutting to the east of the Pont des Quatre Vaux. The battery was at once switched on to this target, fire being opened at the lowest range that would clear the crest (1400 yards), fuse 2½. Section fire was

---

23. Solid masses of German infantry were noticed advancing down a valley between Forest and Neuvilly towards the Selle. They came under our artillery fire, apparently the 60-pdrs. The loss inflicted was considerable, but it was not sufficient to arrest the forward flow of the blocks of infantry.

ordered at the best rate that could be kept up. Owing to the heavy casualties that had occurred in the detachments the fire was necessarily slow and ragged—but it was effective.[24] The proof being that during the entire action this frontal attack never progressed beyond the cutting.

Before the end of this period the telephone wires connecting the B.C. and his guns were cut to shreds by shell-fire. An attempt was then made to replace this method of communication by flag-signalling, but the signallers in the battery at once became casualties. To keep up the connection was vital, so a chain of orderlies was used to link up the right section with the O.P. These men lay out in the open under a heavy fire, in order that their battery should not fail the infantry at the crisis, which all could see was fast approaching.[25] In this connection it is permissible to quote the testimony of the officer commanding the 2/Suffolk Regiment, which the XV and 37 (Hows.) were immediately supporting:—

> I should like to place on record the more than excellent work done by the four batteries under Lt.-Col. C. F. Stevens, R.F.A.; their behaviour throughout was magnificent and the moral effect on us was great. In spite of being enfiladed first from left and then from right they continued to fire; and though some had better targets than others all behaved with the greatest coolness under the most trying circumstances. From my trench I could see Major Birley, 80 R.F.A., giving his orders as if it were an ordinary field-day. In a position where a wrongly set fuse involved great loss of life to us I think I am right in saying that there was not a single premature during the whole day from the twenty-four guns—surely a wonderful feat.[26]

---

24. The C.O. of the German 72nd Infantry Regiment (8th Division, IV Corps), the regiment that carried out the frontal attack on our right flank at Le Cateau, visited Torgau in 1914. He informed our officers, who were imprisoned there, that his regiment had lost heavily on 26th August. The rifle-fire of the companies of the 2 K.O.Y.L.I. along the Roman Road (*vide* Sketch B.) played its part in the infliction of this punishment. The western bank of the Roman Road being higher than the eastern, two tiers of fire were possible.

25. By this time in the exposed battery O. P. the battery sergeant major had been severely wounded and the look-out man (a sergeant) had been killed.

26. By Maj. E. C. Doughty: he succeeded to the command of 2/Suff. R.. after Lt.-Col. Brett, D.S.O. had been killed early in the action. It is pleasing to record that the artillery all bear witness to the magnificent behaviour of the 2/Suff. R., through the long ordeal to which it was subjected.

On the right (eastern) flank the guns were less than 100 yards behind the trenches occupied by the Suffolks, whilst on the left flank not more than 200 yards separated them. The deafening roar made by the continual detonation of the German high-explosive among the guns and trenches was increased by the noise of our guns replying to their fire, rendering communication most difficult in the Suffolks' trenches. "There was a continual roar of fire." At least two machine gun batteries kept the crest of the ridge under a continuous fire, delivered at decisive range; but this fire was not very effective in the batteries and here most of the damage was done by gunfire.

Meanwhile XXVIII had been very heavily engaged by the German artillery, though they still failed to locate 122. As the German infantry lines showed, advancing over the crests of the rolling ground from 2,400 to 1,300 yards from the battery's position, they were fired on with good effect.[27] All the while the battery was under rifle (or machine gun?) fire from the spur near Pont des Quatre Vaux.[28]

123 had been located by the Germans and they did their best to destroy it as well as the four guns of 124 which were in action in the open immediately behind it. A very heavy fire was concentrated on these two batteries, but the guns were fought on and as Infantry targets presented themselves they were very effectively engaged. The appearance given by the advance of the German infantry was groups of four or five lines, one behind the other, advancing at a time. The men in each line were extended to about a pace interval, possibly 50 yards between fines, with 200 yards in depth separating one group of lines from another.[29]

Given such a target the batteries dealt out destruction to it that went far to repay the losses they were suffering. Nor did the enemy in this part ever show any desire to advance beyond the line of the Cambrai Road whilst the guns were waiting for them.

The damage done, however, to 123 and 124 was considerable. In

---

27. The target generally appeared to be a platoon extended shoulder to shoulder. One round gunfire was sufficient for its destruction. The whole platoon would go down "like a target at practice-camp when the rope is cut."

28. Major A. S. Peebles. D.S.O., who became 2nd in command of 2 Suff. R.. after the C.O. was killed, located at least 9 German machine guns in the deep cutting to the east of Pont des Quatre Vaux. They did an enormous amount of damage. Capt. E. E. Orford of the same regiment also noticed and fired at others along the Cambrai read to the west of Pont des Quatre Vaux.

29. Further details of the German infantry's attack formations on Aug. 26th would be very valuable.

123, No. 3 was put out of action by a direct hit and at least two of the wagons were set on fire. 124 was in much the same plight; two guns were silenced by direct hits and two wagons were alight. Nevertheless the available ammunition began to run low and an attempt was made about noon to bring up more, but it was impossible to get it through under the heavy gun fire that was opened on the batteries.[30]

In this part of the field also the pounding was excessive, but even so the three batteries never failed to give to their Infantry every possible support and co-operation.

Immediately to the west the strain was much less severe. 119 obtained some effect against German infantry beyond the main Cambrai road, but its held of fire was small and the enemy was not pressing on. In this period the battery was unfavourably placed for effective work, consequently about noon it was ordered back to a position about one mile to the north of Reumont where it could fire with far greater effect against the advancing infantry.

121 remained in its original position and fired heavily and with effect against the German infantry. 120, which co-operated with the Third Division, pushed a section to the west of Troisvilles to flank any advance from Beaumont, and these guns caused considerable losses to the Germans as they left the village in their attempt to advance against the centre of the line,

65 (Hows.), co-operating with XXVII, bombarded the villages of Inchy and Beaumont setting them on fire. The battery noticed three well marked attacks in its section of the front. All broke down under the fire with which they were greeted, 65 (Hows.) materially assisting in beating off two attacks on Troisvilles. In these repulses the rifle must also have had its share.

The Reserve Artillery, meanwhile, had not been inactive. 61 (Hows.) searched localities using the map, useful results being reported; whilst 108 Heavy Battery dealt with any targets that offered. The light had improved steadily as the morning wore on and the 60-pdrs. were able to deal with German guns in action near Croix[31] and also with some batteries nearer at hand.

The fire of the former ceased almost immediately, but the latter tried, ineffectually, to find the Heavy Battery. Towards noon it became

---

30. XXVIII P.A.C. issued 168,000 rounds S.A.A. to the 14th Inf. Bde. Reserve, and 8 wagons of 18-pdr. ammunition to XXVIII.

31. At 9.2.5 a.m. one of our observers saw 3 German brigades of artillery in action close to the Montay—Croix road. (*Vide* chapter 3).

necessary to shift the battery O.P. to a less exposed position about 300 yards to the right flank of the guns.[32]

The Fifth D.A.C. was ordered at noon to take post at the road junction north-west of Fremont and to be ready to supply ammunition as needed.

Thus against the right section of this part of the front the Germans were evidently concentrating their greatest effort.[33] Even so the batteries of the defence had not been silenced before the German infantry showed up and then the fire they poured in, from those guns that could still be fought, took a heavy toll from the assailants. It was not to be mere child's play for the attackers despite their preponderance in guns.

The greeting accorded to the German infantry caused the enemy to abandon temporarily the projected onslaught, and once more to have recourse to his numerically superior artillery in order to open the way for his infantry to close, without suffering too heavy a loss.[34]

(b) Third Division—(See Map 3).

Opposite to this part of the line large bodies of the German infantry did not show up as much as they did against the right flank, and in advancing they used the available cover with considerable skill. [35] However, they were reported massing in several localities which were promptly shelled; and the wood east of Bethencourt was subjected to a heavy crossfire by XXIII and XL when German infantry were using its leafy shade to camouflage their concentration. Indeed by 9 a.m. our batteries were seriously engaged and firing was practically continuous. By this hour the German guns had also opened fire and

32. It is interesting to note that A coy., 2/Duke of Wellington's R. (about 100 strong), had been detailed as an escort to the Heavy Battery and it formed up in the hollow alongside the Roman Road.

33. According to one estimate about 100 German guns were massed against the 2/ Suffolks and XV R.F.A.

34. Our air-reports for this period furnish the following information about German troops who were confronting the Fifth Division:—By 9.35 a.m. Le Cateau was on fire in several places, but the town was clear of troops. At noon fires were still noticeable in the place. It was soon afterwards that the same observer saw a heavy German column about six miles long (possibly a division) marching down the Roman Road. It had reached Englefontaine. This column would probably arrive on the battlefield at the critical moment of the action, when its intervention on the German side might prove decisive in the wavering fight against the outnumbered and hard-pressed Fifth Division.

35. The German infantry advancing across the rolling downs to Inchy were extended at about 3 to 1 paces between files, the lines being about 100 yds. apart.

were engaged in pounding the ridge and all likely gun positions. But our batteries were skilfully placed and comparatively little damage was done to them.

109 kept a sunken road, west of Inchy, under a steady fire, and as long as the battery remained in action the German infantry failed to advance beyond this line.

XL kept in action despite the heavy fire concentrated on them, it shelled the Bethencourt wood with good effect, whilst 23 and 49 dealt with German infantry who were visible between 3,000 and 2,000 yards away. At 11 a.m. 129 (Hows.) moved back into a position close to Montigny; but the rest of their doings in this period are veiled in obscurity.

XLII was unable to find a satisfactory position near Tronquoy, as the batteries would have been open to enfilade from the northwest. The brigade then moved through Montigny and came into action to the west of that village. Here it was unable to fire as the range was excessive during this phase.

41 was now brought into action at the north-east end of the small copse alongside which it had been hidden. [36] It registered, and then it remained in observation waiting for a target. The Battery had been specially ordered to be ready to cover Ligny in case of necessity.

48 Heavy Battery was busily engaged in shelling advancing infantry, who at these longer ranges gave more promising targets, as well as in searching the ground from which the Infantry appeared, to prevent any concentration prior to attack. It was also employed on counter-battery work controlling the German batteries as far as possible.

XL B.A.C., passing through Elincourt, found the Third D.A.C. at the fork roads immediately to the west of that place and proceeded to refill. It was about 10 a.m. Immediately afterwards a staff officer arrived and ordered the B.A.C. to move back to the Third Division, as the Second Corps was fighting. The column at once moved towards the battlefield, and taking up a position north of Clary, about 11 a.m., it made arrangements to issue ammunition.

From 10 a.m. to noon the action raged in this section though never so fiercely as on the right flank. The German heavy (5.9") howitzers freely used high explosive shell. The moral effect of a sudden outburst from these weapons was very great, particularly on troops in villages[37] and buildings; but during this phase the batteries of the Third Divi-

36. *Vide Errata.*

37. Both Audencourt and Caudry were heavily shelled by 5.9".

sion, being well concealed, suffered comparatively slight loss.[38]

(c) Fourth Division—(See Map 4).

Here on the left flank the artillery duel was the principal feature until noon. Meanwhile, about 9.30 a.m., a position having been found for 135, of XXXII, to the north of Ligny, suitable for the close defence of that place in conjunction with the 11th Infantry Brigade, the battery was brought into action in sections which were entrenched behind the hedges to the north and north-east of the village. Although dispersed the sections were fairly close together, a double line of communications connecting the centre and left sections whilst the right section (which later had one of its guns near the station) was supervised by the captain. Two wagons were placed with each gun and the teams were kept in readiness among the houses.

The village of Ligny was a very important point. Its loss, as well as jeopardising the position held by the Fourth Division, would affect the Third Division quite as materially. Once the Germans occupied this village they could enfilade all the ground round Tronquoy and Montigny. It was essential to hold the village, and the arrangement to allot guns for its close defence was obviously a sound one.

To the west of Ligny 27 knocked out a machine gun for the 11th Infantry Brigade; but the Germans immediately opened so many batteries on it that the ammunition could not be replenished, and when it was nearly exhausted the detachments were withdrawn until the storm subsided. By this time the Germans had put a direct hit. on the under shield of No. 5. Soon after a pause occurred and ammunition was replenished in all the wagons, being brought up by hand along the road in rear, and the wheels of No. 5 were replaced from the wagon body. Later on 27 was ordered to cover the retirement of our infantry, but the battery was unsuitably placed to carry out this task.[39] As our infantry in front fell back 27 opened on a German battery in action close to the one it had knocked out earlier in the morning. But this activity drew down an intense return fire from a Heavy as well as from

---

38. About 10 a.m. an observer in one of our aeroplanes noticed that considerable numbers of German troops were on the move near Viesly. Another reported that by noon Caudry was on fire; and the same officer also noticed that Le Quesnoy was full of troops. Later when flying over Blaugies (south-east of Dour) he saw that the place was blocked by German transport; very properly he found the target a tempting one and threw some bombs among the vehicles.

39. The original position was not selected with this idea; it was obviously impossible to change it after the action opened.

two field batteries. An infantry brigade major now came up to the B.C. and said that the battery, by drawing the German fire on to itself, was doing just what the infantry wanted.

The battery managed to keep in action until its ammunition ran out. Then, as no more could be brought up, the men were once again withdrawn under cover.

XXXVII (Hows.) did not fire from their first position and it was not long before the Howitzer Brigade moved back a short distance to a better position in the valley to the east of Selvigny. The sector allotted to this brigade was to the eastward of a north-south line through Haucourt.[40] Soon after XXXVII had taken up. its position Lieut.-Colonel Battiscombe saw a German officer, followed by an orderly carrying a black and white flag, gallop along the crest of the spur beyond the Warnelle Ravine. The batteries were warned. Presently some gun-teams appeared and directly afterwards gun-shields were seen. A howitzer battery at once opened fire and smothered the German guns, and the latter never got off a single round.

XXIX and XIV maintained their original positions and continued their activity.

Beyond the left flank the pressure had been slight. Except 27, which was in action in an exposed position, the artillery of the Fourth Division were practically intact at the end of this phase and ready for any eventuality.

(d) Royal Horse Artillery.

III R.H.A. "D" remained in the positions already indicated.

In VII R.H.A. "L" detached two sections which moved out and occupied two positions in front.[41] During this phase the battery fired some rounds at long ranges, possibly to assist the cavalry engaged on the spur to the south of Le Cateau.

"I" moved south with XLII and took up a position of observation north of Montigny. This was found to be so open to enfilade from the north-west that the battery limbered up almost immediately and moved through Montigny with XLII, finally coming into action

---

40. During this phrase the air-reports furnish the following information about the German troops opposed to the Fourth Division:—About 11 a.m. a German brigade was seen in position to the S.E. of Douai. Soon afterwards the same observer noticed 2 Cavalry Regiments halted in the fields about 1 mile to the east of Cambrai, whilst a German division was in line facing S.S.E., astride the *chaussée* to the north of Wambaix.

41. Possibly one was covering the approaches from S. Souplet.

about 1000 yards west of that village. "I" remained here until 3 p.m.

SUMMARY.

Thus this important period came to an end. During the morning the numerous German batteries had unlimbered on a far-flung, sweeping arc that enveloped the whole British position, and then they proceeded to smother the whole line where the Second Corps stood so grimly at bay under that August sun. But the British batteries responded resolutely, roaring defiance at the German guns, spreading death and destruction among their infantry, proving once and for all that, in 1914, as a killing weapon the 18-pdr. had no equal in Europe.

(C). THE CRISIS OF THE ACTION. NOON TO 1.45 P.M.

(a) Fifth Division—(See Map 2 and Sketch B.)

The German artillery gradually wore down XV and the batteries had great difficulty in keeping any guns in action. An officer of the 18th Hussars, who was near S. Souplet, described the pounding that our right flank was subjected to, as follows:—

> The whole spur was churned up by the German shells, and the earth was thrown about as if by a succession of mines.

Early in this phase the B.C. of 52 was wounded in his O.P.[42] being shot through the throat. Captain Barber Starkey had just arrived at the O.P. to inform the B.C. of the situation in his battery. When Major Nutt had regained consciousness and was able to whisper faintly he sent his captain back into the battery to keep up the best possible rate of fire. From this time onwards the only target that could be engaged was advancing infantry, passing from the wood (north-west of Le Cateau) to the deep cutting; and, although the fuse was decreased to 2, yet no shorter range than 1400 yards was possible, owing to the difficulty of clearing the crest. Major Nutt remained in his O.P. to observe the effect and control the fire.

About half-past one the signallers of 37 (Hows.) passed up to XV Brigade O.P. a message ordering the retirement of the guns. Considering the only orders he had received previously, Lieut.-Colonel Stevens decided he could not act on a mere signal message, and as far as he could ascertain the right flank was still capable of sustaining the action for some time longer.

---

42. The O.P. of 52 was not with that of the XV R.F.A. and 37 (Hows.) but a short distance (about 10 yards) in front of the latter.

At the close of this period, 11 was out of action; 80 had at least two guns firing and had expended more than the ammunition carried in its original six wagons; 37 (Hows.) were still in action as a battery and had fired away nearly all the ammunition in both wagon lines; whilst 52 had the two flank guns still stubbornly responding to the German fire. By the close of the action this battery had fired about 1,100 rounds. [43]

The teams and wagon lines of these four batteries had to change their position more than once, as the German artillery constantly searched for them in the upper valley. As the fight wore on both men and horses suffered heavy casualties from this cause; and the commanding officer of the 59th Field Company, Royal Engineers, who was on a spur to the east of Reumont, stated that:

> One of the saddest things I have seen was the wounded horses trying to keep themselves on their legs by leaning against the stooks of corn.

Immediately to the west of the Roman Road 122 was probably in the best case of all the batteries in these two brigades, its only difficulty being the replenishment of ammunition. [44] 123 had still three of its guns in action and they were firing until the end. The B.C. (Captain Gillman) observed from a position in the open cornfield on the spur to the west of his battery. It was during this phase that he noticed the German infantry pressing forward on his left front and only about a quarter of a mile away, so he went down into the battery to warn the section commanders of what was impending and to make the necessary arrangements for meeting the attack.

The left section was run round to receive the infantry with a point-blank burst of fire directly it showed. The German infantry, however, was driven back by an advance made by our infantry and 123 was not called upon to intervene. Regularly every hour from the time he took over Captain Gillman walked slowly up and down his battery, speaking to all the detachments, whilst salvoes of H.E. and shrapnel were poured in from no less than three German batteries.

In 124 two guns were kept in action, the other two had been silenced by direct hits and at least two wagons were on fire. It will give

---

43. The Ammunition Expenditure on Aug. 26th is dealt with in Appendix 4.
44. During the last phase of the action the B.C. noticed that immediately after 122 had been active the German batteries at once responded by plastering 123 and 124 with shell.

some idea of the nature of the German fire to which XXVIII was subjected when it is realised that a subaltern of 123 stated that he was quite unconscious of the fire of 124, although every round fired by the right section of that battery must have passed within eight feet above his head. 124 never fired a premature all day.

In XXVII all the batteries were still in action and 65 (Hows.) were particularly active against the German infantry who were now providing the principal targets. By the end of this period 65 had fired 840 rounds and being unable to get any more ammunition the battery stood fast awaiting further orders. The howitzers were so well concealed that they had never been located and the few casualties suffered were the result of chance bullets and shells.

The two batteries in Divisional Reserve—61 (Hows.) and 108 Heavy Battery—were actively employed during the period; but they were shortly to be given a far better chance of exhibiting their powers of destruction.

From the foregoing it will be realised that the B.A.C's must have been actively employed in replenishing the battery wagons; and to re-fill the B.A.C's themselves as rapidly as possible the Fifth D.A.C., from the neighbourhood of Prémont, transferred ammunition to some of the motor lorries of the Ammunition Park in which it was rushed up to Reumont (5 miles away) in 20 minutes. The system worked admirably.

Unfortunately some of the shell sent up for the howitzers, as well as some for the 60-pdrs., were short of fuses and a bag of fuses had to be fetched by a motorcyclist; luckily the mistake was repaired in time.

The result of the extreme pressure exerted on the Fifth Division during this phase can be gauged from the messages which were sent into Corps Headquarters. At 12.58 p.m. the corps was informed that if the pressure on the right flank was not soon diminished there was a grave risk that "it may go". At 1.15 p.m. a strong German force, about a division, was reported to be moving wide round the right flank; and at 1.20 p.m. the divisional commander considered that it was a question whether he had better not start retiring at once, unless material assistance could be rendered to his division.

To meet this critical situation on the right there was only the General Reserve of two battalions, 19th Infantry Brigade, that had moved to Montigny earlier in the day. So far they had not been employed; and now, as the crisis was obviously at hand, the corps ordered back these two battalions from Montigny to Bertry. At 1.40 p.m. the Fifth Division was informed by the corps that directly these two battalions reached Bertry they would be sent on at once to Reumont, and would thus be available to reinforce the threatened right or to cover its withdrawal. But some considerable time must elapse before they could be expected to reach Reumont. The Third Division were also asked if they could spare any artillery to assist the Fifth Division, but no batteries were now available for this task.

It is clear that on the right flank and right centre of the Fifth Division the enemy had gained sufficient artillery preponderance to warrant him in risking another immediate overwhelming attack with his infantry.[45] To meet it there were on the ground only a comparatively few guns left in action and the ammunition supply in the exposed Batteries was almost exhausted. But the Germans remembered only too well the rapid fire of the British infantry on August 23 and 24 and they made no attempt to rush the position.

(b) Third Division—(See Map 3).

In the centre a general lull in the German fire was noticeable between noon and 1 p.m.[46] It gave rise to various ideas, either that the enemy were beaten off, or that they were completing their arrangements before the delivery of the final assault. Probably never having intended to drive in the centre, and finding it too well placed and too strong to carry without disproportionate loss, they shifted what guns and troops they could to the east, in order to concentrate enough troops there to make certain of overwhelming the British right flank.

At 1 p.m. the action broke out again with great violence; apparently the crisis on the right was fast approaching. By 1.30 p.m. the Third Division reported to the corps that an attack was developing against Inchy.

All the batteries were still in action, and they remained actively engaged, with the exception of the two forward sections in XXIII which had been ordered to withhold their fire and wait until the German infantry commenced its advance up the vulnerable re-entrants on the forward slope of the Audencourt ridge. Shortly after noon a

---

45. About noon the platoon commander stationed in the front trench of A Company, 1/E. Surrey R. (to the east of the Roman Road) saw the Germans unlimber two heavy guns on the 150 metre knoll immediately in front of our right flank. These guns engaged our batteries at about 2,000 yards range. The officer could distinctly see the detachments serving the guns.

46. This lull has not yet been traced either in the Fifth or Fourth Divisional areas.

message reached the forward section of 108 that German infantry in Inchy were becoming engaged with the 9th Infantry Brigade. The section at once commenced to sweep in front of the village.[47] Immediately afterwards some of our howitzers (unidentified) turned on to the village with H. E.[48] The German infantry were held.

An officer[49] of XL B.A.C. describes his impression of the battlefield, at 2 p.m., as follows:—

> I was standing on the northern edge of Bertry. To my front lay the open Caudry ridge beyond which showed the dark line of trees along the Cambrai road. I could see our batteries strung out in an irregular line and all were in action firing hard. Shrapnel flecked the whole landscape and in the village of Audencourt heavy high explosives were bursting on percussion among the houses.
>
> But the din of battle was dominated by the throb of noise from our right flank. We all looked instinctively in the direction of Le Cateau where the Montay spur was overhung by a bank of white and yellow smoke, punctuated by angry flashes.

Between noon and 2 p.m. the B.A.Cs. of XXX (Hows.), XL, and XLII were along the road between Montigny and Clary. In the Third D.A.C. all the ammunition was used in replenishment, some of the sections even sending wagons directly up to the Batteries themselves. The ground permitted this re-supply to be carried out in the Third Division and no ammunition shortage is reported by any batteries of the division.

Thus in this area the strain had not been felt unduly; the line here had not been really tested, and there was nothing to indicate any necessity for retirement.[50]

(c) Fourth Division—(See Map 4.)

In this division the artillery remained in action although more severely tried than in the Third Division. At 12.10 p.m. the division was able to report to the Second Corps that "my guns are keeping

---

47. The section of 108 was entrenched in a root-field, and all newly-turned soil as well as the gun-shields and the wagons had been camouflaged thoroughly with turnip-tops. Shortly before noon rifle bullets commenced to patter against the shields although so far no hostile infantry had been observed in Inchy.

48. This may have been 65 (Hews.) of the Fifth Division.

49. Captain (then Lieut.) C. A. L. Brownlow, D.S.O.

50. This is evident when the casualties of this division are studied, *vide* Appendix 3.

down the fire on Ligny".[51] At that time the village was held by the six guns of 135, together with 200 men and two machine guns. 135 were engaged by two German field guns which were run up by hand close to Fontaine-au-pire, only 2,500 yards away. A section was at once turned on to them and eight shrapnel sufficed for the business, numerous casualties being observed. Any attempt made by the German infantry to advance was heavily punished by this battery, and no attack on Ligny was pressed home whilst 135 remained in action. The rolling down in its front gave the battery an ideal chance to smash up any infantry advance and it was quick to avail itself of it. The sections had been very skilfully concealed and were never located by the German artillery.

During the afternoon, the sky becoming overcast, the brigade commander went up to the guns of 27 with the B.C., but any movement there at once drew down a heavy fire and all idea of getting them out before dark was temporarily abandoned. Later they were again visited, when it was found that the trails were so deeply embedded that they could not be lifted until the earth around them had been loosened.

Two batteries of XXXVII (Hows.)—31 and 55—engaged German artillery from their new positions, but no results could be ascertained. The enemy responded but the shell were chiefly over and no serious damage was done, though the German shooting improved after two aeroplanes had flown over the brigade; but even so the howitzers were never accurately located. Towards the close of this phase German infantry were seen advancing in strength across the ridge north of Longsart and two of the howitzer batteries opened on them at ranges varying from 4,500 to 3,500 yards. Our infantry reported that considerable effect was obtained. Probably with the idea of supporting this attack the Germans had placed one or more machine guns in the Moulin d'Esnes and their fire was particularly galling to the two companies of the 2/Royal Inniskilling Fusiliers that held Esnes. The mill was set on fire—probably by the howitzers—to the great relief of the infantry.

About this time 68 and 39 fell back to a position alongside 88, and the whole of XIV was then in action to the east of S. Aubert Fme.[52]

---

51. In the same message the division said that, "the cable cart you sent us is most useful." In this way the disadvantage of being without its Signal Company was partially overcome During the action the Third D.A.C. assisted the Fourth Division, in the absence of the Fourth D.A.C.

52. It was probably here that Major R. England, Commanding 88, was killed. though the time is not certain.

In this section, as in that of the Third Division, nothing had occurred to shake the hold of the troops on their position, which they could certainly have maintained until dark, had it been necessary to do so and had not the situation on the right flank dictated otherwise.[53]

(d) Royal Horse Artillery—(See Map 5.)

All that can be gleaned about this period from the available diaries and sources is that, probably about 1 p.m., "D" R.H.A. was withdrawn from its position near Bazuel and that the battery then moved back past S. Benin.

Fortunately the Germans proved unenterprising and did not occupy the S. Benin spur. "D", meanwhile, was held in reserve ready to cover the eventual retirement of "E" and "L", which were in action covering the Honnechy valley.

Summary.

Favoured as they were by circumstances, the ground, the open nature of our right flank, the lack of reserves in the Second Corps, as well as by their own crushing superiority m guns, machine guns, and men, the Germans had concentrated their main effort against the two brigades holding the extreme right flank of the British line; and as a result of eight hours fighting they had placed that flank in critical danger.

But the action fought by the Second Corps on August 26th was only a delaying one and if the necessary time had now been gained then the moment to retire had come. Otherwise a disaster to the right must be faced and that might easily involve the rest of the force, for as yet there were still left many hours of daylight.

(D). The Retirement—After 1.45 p.m. [54]

---

53. About 1 p.m. an observer in one of our aeroplanes saw that Cambrai was occupied by the Germans and he noticed the usual traces of their handiwork in the town, fires had started. At about 1.30 p.m. the engine of the aeroplane was unluckily damaged by a bullet, but the pilot effected a glide of two miles and managed to land among some of the French cavalry who were retreating towards Arras. The pilot and observer were fortunate enough to obtain two bicycles and later a motorcar, and thus made their way to S. Quentin. They reached the place about 11.30 p.m., and at once proceeded to report to the G.O.C., Second Corps.

54. At 1.30 p.m. the Fifth Division reported that the right flank was seriously attacked, but the G.O.C. was ordered to hold on as long as possible. At the same time the situation was communicated to the other divisions and all were warned, if retirement became imperative, that the Fifth Division would give the order. In that case the Third Division was to conform whilst the (continued next page),

(a) Fifth Division—(See Map 2 and Sketch B).

By 1.45 p.m. the situation on the right flank had reached a critical stage. German machine guns were now solidly established along the line of the Cambrai road, within 500 yards of the infantry firing line. Further, owing to their great numerical superiority, the German guns had at last gained an ascendancy over XV and XXVIII R.F.A., whilst the German infantry, in possession of Le Cateau and the big spur above the railway station, were steadily pouring round the open right flank of the 2/Suffolk Regiment and XV R.F.A.

Many guns were out of action, a few owing to direct hits; others failed to run up properly owing to the rapid fire maintained, or to dents in the buffers; others ceased firing owing to casualties among the detachments; others were silent through shortage of ammunition. The time had come to retire and orders were now issued about 2 p.m. to withdraw the guns.

When the C.R.A. considered that XV had been practically silenced he ordered his brigade major to collect the teams and arrange for the withdrawal of the guns. Major Tailyour accompanied the teams of XV R.F.A.[55] It was decided not to attempt the withdrawal of 52, as the battery was in such an exposed situation and, its wagon line having been heavily shelled after the German artillery had worked round the right flank, the losses in horses had been considerable. The remaining teams were used to assist in recovering 37 (Hows.) and 80. At the time when their respective limbers arrived, although 11 had been definitely silenced, yet two guns of 80, 37 (Hows.), and the flank guns of 52 were all still firing; indeed the last mentioned guns continued in action until the end.

The arrival of the teams was quite unexpected in the batteries. As the situation was critical and it was quite impossible to keep the teams waiting in the open, as many guns as possible were limbered up at once and driven off. It seems probable that the teams of 11 were the first to reach the line of guns; in their advance one team had been shot down but the other five guns were successfully limbered up and

---

Fourth Division covered the operation. The necessary roads for the movement had been allotted to the divisions. Between 2.30 and 3 p.m. news was received at Corps H.Q. at Bertry that the Fifth Division had been compelled to fall back. (From H.Q. Diary, II Corps).

55. Major Tailyour apparently reached Col. Stevens and was captured with him. The account in the C.R.A's Diary has been followed. Other and later evidence tends to show that Maj. Tailyour led forward the limbers of 80 and 37 (Hows) himself. They galloped down the valley and Major Tailyour sent the limbers of 80 to that battery leading those of 37 up to the howitzers.

started off.[56] The B.C. (who had been wounded) rode back on one of the limbers, but unfortunately this gun overturned in the valley below and consequently only four of the six guns were saved. Major Henning finally got back to Reumont on a gun of 80, which apparently came out of action some time after 11 had retired.[57] Major Birley having sent off his battery was on his way [58] to the Brigade O.P. to report to the brigade commander, but he was wounded at once and on proceeding to Reumont was again hit.

These daring attempts were surprisingly successful; four guns of 11, five of 80, and four howitzers of 37, were driven away and saved. Possibly a brief lull that occurred in the shelling, just as the limbers of 80 and 37 reached the guns, was accountable for the success that was achieved. Nevertheless two teams were blown to pieces as they came up and it was only after great efforts that the guns were extricated; in some cases, where there were not sufficient gunners available, the drivers promptly dismounted and assisted in the limbering up. The survivors of the batteries now disabled the remaining guns and withdrew from them carrying most of the wounded with them. It was high time they retired. The German infantry were closing inexorably round the right flank of the 2/Suffolk Regiment and the machine gun bullets were coming through the gun-shields.

The Germans were now determined to assault, and masses of their infantry suddenly appeared out of the sunken road behind the right flank of the line held by the 2/Suffolk Regiment. The occupants of these trenches, a mixed force consisting of men belonging to the 2/Suffolk Regiment, 2/Argyll and Sutherland Highlanders, 1/Dorset Regiment, and R.F.A., promptly opened rapid fire on the mass and did so much execution that, instead of rushing the small British force, the German infantry halted and returned the fire, some blazing away from the hip whilst others dropped on their knees before they an-

---

56. Further details are still required about the withdrawal of 11. One of the guns of this battery was lying overturned in the cutting (immediately to the light flank of the battery) and was seen there by a supporting party of the 2/Argyll and Sutherland Highlanders as they advanced some time before noon into the southern trenches of the 2/Suffolk Regiment. It seems that after 11 was practically silenced, some gunners of that battery took rifles and ammunition and went into one of the trenches held by the 2/Suffolk Regiment.

57. The O.P., in which were Col. Stevens and Major Jones, was out of sight of the guns and these officers were informed that horses had been brought up for them; but Col. Stevens considered his duty was to remain.

58. He had been observing in the open close to his guns.

swered. The appearance of these German troops behind our right flank did something to mitigate the machine gun fire from the guns concealed in the Pont des Quatre Vaux cutting, as the enemy realised that most of this fire must take effect on his own infantry.

Seeing that the two abandoned howitzers of 37 must fall into German hands within a few minutes, if they were left where they were, Captain D. Reynolds of the Battery obtained permission from the C.R.A. to call for volunteers to rescue them. Accompanied by Lieutenants E. G. Earle and W. D. Morgan (both belonging to the 37th Battery) Captain Reynolds led up two teams to bring out the howitzers. As they galloped down the valley towards the battery position the German infantry were commencing to swarm all over the ground on which the right batteries of the line had been in action. Nevertheless both howitzers were limbered up, but then one team was shot down by the German infantry who now were not more than two hundred yards away. The other howitzer, however, galloped off and, although one driver was hit, it was brought away.[59]

The C.R.A. saw this episode himself, and personally ordered one of our batteries to stop firing in order to allow Captain Reynolds to make his attempt. For saving this howitzer Captain Reynolds and Drivers Luke and Drain, all of 37, were awarded the Victoria Cross, Lieutenant Earle, who was wounded, received the D.S.O., and the sergeant and the trumpeter were given the D.C.M. It was done only just in time. Directly afterwards, at 2.45 p.m., the German vice closed round the doomed right flank and the 2nd/Suffolk Regiment was overwhelmed.

The following description of the closing scene on the British right flank is from an eyewitness, Lieut.-Col. Stevens, commanding XV R.F.A.:—

About 2.40 p.m. some cheering was heard on our right, about 300 yards away and over the crest. About five minutes afterwards we heard 'Stand Fast!' and 'Cease Fire!' sounded and whistles blown. Then it was shouted down the line from the right, 'You are firing on friends.' All firing stopped at once. On standing upright and looking just over the crest we found everyone standing up and the firing line being rounded up by the

---

59. An officer of the 1/Norfolk R. (15th Inf. Bde.), then engaged in holding the northern perimeter of Reumont to cover the retirement of the Fifth Division, saw Capt. Reynolds advance and return with a gun. He considered this took place between 3 and 3.15 p.m. Any confirmation of the exact time would be most valuable.

Germans. The position was lost, considerable numbers of the enemy being round our right and right rear.

Some time before the end the two right platoons of the 2/Suffolk Regiment had to face about as the Germans had worked right round behind them. Without exaggeration it may be said of the gallant 2/12th enduring to the end at Le Cateau—"*Ils furent vaincus avec honneu.*"

By their behaviour at Le Cateau on August 26 the 2/Suffolk Regiment,[60] and those men of the 2/Argyll and Sutherland Highlanders and 2/Manchester Regiment who had reached the advanced trenches during the action to reinforce the Suffolks, proved they were as worthy of the title of "*immobile infanterie Britannique*" as were the men of Waterloo.

The end of 52 R.F.A. must now be given, it was not an inglorious one. As this phase wore on the fire of the battery became more and more intermittent, single guns firing at long intervals. The battery was in its death-throes. More than once the B.C. must have thought his guns were silenced. But through the devoted gallantry of the wounded the two flank guns were able to maintain a desultory fire. Captain Barber Starkey and a wounded sergeant served one gun, taking it in turns to bring up ammunition from a neighbouring wagon [61].

Finally at 2.45 p.m. the end came with startling suddenness and the flank was overwhelmed and rolled up from the right and right rear. It was impossible to fire into the surging crowd of friends and foes,

60. Attached to the 2/Suffolk Regiment during the whole action were a party of details who had become separated from their own units—26 men of the l/Dorset Regiment. 2 men of the 1/Bedford Regiment, and 6 men of the R.F.A. (the latter were unarmed). This party had been handed over early that morning by the B.G.C. 14th Infantry Brigade, to the CO., 2/Suffolk Regiment. These men fought all day with the 2/Suffolk Regiment and shared its fate.

61. Captain Barber Starkey was severely wounded in performing this duty and he died at Le Cateau on 10 September, 1914. Of the three sergeants, who were captured, all were wounded and all remained to the end working the guns. As far as can be ascertained Lieut. Rome (the senior subaltern) went up to the battery O.P. shortly before 2 p.m. to see if an attempt might be made to get the guns away. Bearing in mind the only orders he had received, the B.C. refused permission. During Lieut. Rome's absence from the guns a staff officer arrived and ordered the remaining subaltern (2nd Lieut. Neve) to withdraw the few men who remained unwounded.

Between 2.45 and 3 p.m. some gunners readied the battery and removed the breech-blocks and sights. Actually the Germans do not seem to have come forward and reached the guns themselves until about 5 p.m.

and the O.P. of the dying battery was over-run by the German 26th Infantry Regiment (7th Division, IV Corps).[62] By this time only dead and wounded men were around the guns of the old "Bengal Rocket Troop"[63].

When the guns of XV had been withdrawn an attempt was made to bring out the guns of XXVIII R.F.A. After his brigade major had gone up to XV, the C.R.A. went to XXVIII to ascertain the situation in that part of the field.

XXVIII was in so exposed a situation that the withdrawal of its three batteries was bound to be very difficult; but if it was to be attempted at all then there was no time to be lost. Some time previously Captain R. A. Jones, of 122, had been up in the battery, but no arrangements for limbering up were made because retirement entered into no one's calculations. Later on,[64] after his return to the wagonline, he received the order to retire the guns. Captain Jones at once proceeded to make adequate arrangements to carry through this duty. First of all he called for volunteers and six teams were immediately obtained. Then he explained the situation to the drivers who were to accompany him and he ordered them, should it prove impossible to limber up, that they should get as close to the guns as possible so as to replenish the ammunition by hand, for it was running short.

Captain Jones then led his teams forward. Moving up the reverse slope they drove through the gap left for them in the trenches of the 1/Royal West Kent Regiment, who were in support to this part of the line; and the infantry appreciating the desperate nature of the attempt stood up as the teams passed and cheered them to the echo. "It was a very fine sight!"[65]

With this tribute to their gallantry ringing m their ears they topped the rise and swung on to the shell-smitten, bullet-torn ground in front of the Sunken Road. Immediately the German gunfire redoubled, and

---

62. Other units that have been identified on this right flank were the 66th and 72nd Infantry Regiments, both belonging to the IV Corps.

63. 52 R.F.A. was originally raised in 1816 as No. 7 Troop, Bengal Horse Artillery and became the Rocket Troop. In 1862 the Indian Artilleries were amalgamated with the Royal Artillery, and the battery became "B" Battery, "F" Brigade, Royal Horse Artillery; "G" Battery, "C" Brigade in 1877, and "M" Battery, "A" Brigade in 1882. In 1887 it was converted into a field battery, becoming "T" Battery, 2nd Brigade; and in 1889 it obtained its present designation.

64. Possibly it was shortly before 2 p.m. The arrival of the limbers was quite unexpected in the battery.

65. From an officer of the 1/R.W. Kent Regt.

a storm of machine gun fire swept down on the teams[66] as they made for the battery. Captain Jones was killed at once by a rifle-bullet, "and no man died that day with more glory—yet many died and there was much glory."[67] In the first minute 8 men were killed, 2nd Lieut. R. W. MacLeod and 14 men were wounded, and 20 horses fell. The remaining teams reached the left guns first and an attempt was made to limber them up. The space in rear of the battery was cramped and this made the task even more difficult. One team was shot down in a heap on the road.

However, by dint of great exertions three of the six guns were limbered up. Although wounded, 2nd Lieut. R. W. MacLeod assisted his only surviving team, unhooked the dead lead-horses, hooked in others, and, the wheel-driver being shot, mounted himself and, with a riding lead, a riding centre, and himself in the wheel, the gun galloped out of action up the spur, 2nd Lieut. MacLeod being wounded again before he was clear of the battery.

Of the two other guns limbered up, one team was shot down at once but the other gun won clear away.

Immediately these guns had got away, the teams of 124, under the battery quarter-master-sergeant, came up behind the cutting on the Troisvilles road, to make the attempt to bring out their battery. Whilst looking for a place to cross the road they were ordered away and forbidden to renew the attempt.[68] It was now clear that the remaining guns (16) would have to be abandoned and the C.R.A. personally issued orders to the B.C. of 124 to that effect. Major Kinsman then communicated the order to Captain Gillman. It was obeyed with great reluctance. Indeed Captain Gillman finding that his battery (123) still possessed 16 rounds had them all fired against the Germans. Both batteries now disabled their guns, smashing the sights, and withdrawing the breech blocks. The wounded were then carried up to cover in the Roman road.[69] When both batteries had been put out of action the

66. Probably from some of the machine guns in the cutting by the Pont des Quatre Vaux; possibly some established along the Cambrai road also co-operated.

67. *Napier.* Book XVI, Chap. V.

68. Apparently by Lt.-Col. Cameron, Comdg. XXVIII. An officer of the 1/Norfolk R. (15th Inf. Bde.), then holding the sunken road immediately to the east of the *Arbre*, noticed these teams retiring. He saw the B.Q.M.S. halt the teams and dismount two drivers to adjust their saddles and was immensely impressed by this sight. Captain C. H. Browning, of 121, had been killed much earlier in the action.

69 In the right and most exposed section of 123 there were 4 killed and 8 wounded, including the section commander, Lieut. E. A. Spencer. The Germans obtained three direct hits on the two guns of this section.

detachments were at last withdrawn Captain Gillman carrying back a wounded infantryman (2/K.O.Y.L.I.).

The last to withdraw (after a considerable interval) were the brigade staff and the battery commanders of 122 and 124.[70] Again it was time. It is true that the German infantry were showing no burning desire to advance beyond the line of the Cambrai road in front, but the fate of the right flank was almost sealed and then the right of the 13th Infantry Brigade was bound to be rolled up with great rapidity.

The batteries of XXVII received the order to retire at a rather later hour than those supporting the two right infantry brigades. It was about 3.30 p.m. when the B.G.C. 15th Infantry Brigade gave orders for 121 to fall back; at that time the battery was suffering from the fire of a machine gun on the Cambrai Road. This fire caused some casualties whilst limbering up and three wagon bodies had to be abandoned. The 15th Infantry Brigade and 119 covered the retirement of 121; and then 119 moved back to a position further in rear.

65 (Hows.) noticed a battery withdrawing about 3.30 p.m.[71] and sent an officer for orders. Before his return the brigade commander of VIII (Hows.) arrived and ordered the battery out of action. This was carried out with the loss of a wagon.

The brigade ammunition columns had been in the fields near Reumont. When the retirement was seen to be inevitable they were ordered back. At 3 p.m. the Fifth Divisional Ammunition Column at Fremont received an order to move. So as to clear the Roman Road it commenced to withdraw on S. Quentin moving *via* Brancourt and Ramicourt.

As our infantry started retiring on the right 61 (Hows.) gave them the most effective support. To commence with, a barrage was put down in front of the abandoned infantry trenches. As one strong attacking line, 8 deep, commenced to press forward, it was swept with lyddite—with the happiest results. No more indiscreet German mobs advanced over the crest in front whilst 61 remained in action, and our infantry were not pursued by rifle fire in their retirement. Finally, having fired all its ammunition, 61 was ordered to retire, and as it fell back was lucky enough to get a re-supply of ammunition from two wagons of 37 (Hows.).

108 Heavy Battery also helped to cover the retirement of the in-

---

70. Major Kinsman waited on hoping that teams could be collected for an attempt to save the guns of his battery.
71. Probably it was 121.

fantry by controlling the fire of the German artillery. Between 2 and 3 p.m. the C.R.A. ordered back one section to a covering position in rear near Maurois. Unfortunately, in crossing a temporary bridge over the stream in rear of the battery's position, one of the guns upset, and as it could not be righted it had to be abandoned after twenty minutes work.[72]

From the section still in action, the German infantry could be seen rallying on the crest south-west of Le Cateau. They were careless enough to crowd together within 3,200 yards of the two 60-pdrs., until a lyddite bursting m the middle of the mass dispersed the survivors to the far side of the hill. The guns then dealt with German artillery until the hostile infantry commenced another and more cautions advance. Gradually the latter worked forward within 2,600 yards; it was now 3.30 p.m. and the G.O.C. Fifth Division, ordered the two guns back. To cover the advance of the teams, the 60-pdrs. kept up a steady fire of shrapnel and lyddite; then, limbering up rapidly, trotted out of action and did not check their pace until they were clear of the zone of the German artillery fire.[73]

Without the co-operation of 61 (Hows.) and 108 Heavy Battery the withdrawal of the two right infantry brigades[74] of the Fifth Division would have been a most difficult and costly operation. The handling of these two batteries, at this critical time, went far to save the right flank from being overwhelmed.

The Fifth Division had maintained its position until the very last possible moment, the advanced batteries remaining in support of the infantry firing line until then. Considering the situation, it is surprising that so many guns were saved in the division.[75]

(b) Third Division.—(See Map 3).

It was about 3 p.m. when the 9th Infantry Brigade (on the right of the Third Division) was ordered to retire as the Fifth Division was falling back. XXIII was at once withdrawn, except the two advanced sections—from 107 and 108—entrenched on the forward slope, with 100 rounds per gun available in each section. These guns now came

---

72. From the description of an officer who crossed this stream during the day, the obstacle was formidable, not on account of its width, which was only between 7 and 8 feet, but because it was comparatively deep and had almost perpendicular banks.
73. Apparently 1914 was its first war service; the battery was formed in 1904.
74. XIV and XIII.
75. 47 out of 74, and 16 from the exposed 7 batteries (42 guns). The guns lost are given in Appendix 2.

into action to cover the retirement of the infantry. They shelled the southern edge of Inchy where the German infantry were massing for the assault and blew them back. When the ammunition was all fired away the guns were disabled (for it was impossible to withdraw them)[76] and the detachments retired with the infantry. They had been completely successful for the infantry got back to the guns almost unscathed and then passed out of the enemy's sight, whilst the detachments themselves had no casualties.[77]

XL being further to the west, the order for retirement appears to have reached it rather later.[78] Being in action under cover the Brigade got away without great difficulty; but three of the guns from C R.F.A. had to be left behind.

XLII was in action further back, and it naturally stood its ground to cover the retirement of the foremost brigades. It was only about 4.30 p.m. that it limbered up and moved southward through Montigny. Just before this XXX (Hows.) had preceded it along the same road.

41, from its original position, could now bring effective fire to bear on the Germans who were trying to advance on the western side of Caudry. The battery opened on these targets and apparently remained in action for some time. It eventually withdrew when ordered to do so, and got away without difficulty or loss, although the Audencourt ridge was now definitely in the German possession and the battery had to retire for some distance up the hillside before it could gain any cover.

48 Heavy Battery limbered up without difficulty and withdrew about 4.30 p.m., having been employed in covering the initial stage of

---

76. In 108, 2 guns, 1 gun limber, 1 wagon limber and 2 bodies were left in the pits. In the battery itself the only casualty in the action was one horse wounded; in 109 the only casualties all day were 4 horses hit. The small casualties were eloquent testimony to the placing of these batteries whose fire had been so destructive.

77. It was apparently 3.30 p.m. when the forward section of 108 (under Lieut. E. L. B. Anderson) received the news that a general retirement had been ordered. The section was to cover the withdrawal of all the infantry and retire last of all. At about 4 p.m. the bde. major, 9th Bde., ordered back the 1/Lincoln R. in front of the section of 108 and he was killed as he finished delivering the order. Owing to the fire of the section the 1/Lincoln R. only lost 7 men when withdrawing from their exposed position—proof of the effective fashion in which the German fire was controlled at this critical time. A small party of the 1/Lincoln R. (an officer and 50 men) halted close to the section for a fight to a finish. But the orders to withdraw were explicit and there was nothing for it but to disable the guns thoroughly and join the retiring infantry.

78. The diary says, "4 p.m."

the retirement up to that hour.

At 3.30 p.m. XL Brigade Ammunition Column was ordered to withdraw;[79] but it was not until 5 p.m. that orders reached the Third Divisional Ammunition Column to retire through Serain. Two guns (unidentified)[80] came into action to protect the rear of the divisional ammunition column and the divisional train as they moved off, their progress being slow owing to a mass of vehicles which blocked the road.

A description of the state of the battlefield around Audencourt has been furnished by an artillery officer,[81] who was wounded and captured at Ligny. He was removed on September 1 through Audencourt to a German hospital at Bethencourt. South of the village of Audencourt and in a field to the west of the road he saw some 18-pdr. guns.[82] An unlimbered gun proved that the battery had been in position facing roughly north and large piles of empty cases showed where the guns had stood. One gun was half-way from the position to the gate leading to the road. Another was limbered up in the gate and stood there with the team, all black horses, lying dead in front of it.

Further on, in the village itself, was a medley of water-carts, cable-carts, and general service limbered-wagons, each lying by the roadside with the horses or mules dead in the shafts. At the northern end of the village were four machine guns,[83] their detachments and three officers lying dead beside them. One of the guns was painted in blotches of various colours. The bank of the road at the northern end of the village, a hedgerow about four feet high, was pitted with hastily scraped hollows. Nearly every hollow held its man.

Just to the south of the Le Cateau—Cambrai road and close to it were the remains of a German gun position. One gun, damaged by a direct hit, still stood there, the positions occupied by the others being indicated by five piles of empty cases. A little to the right was a small mound of freshly turned earth with five helmets on the top. These helmets had the artillery ball, in place of the spike, and were obviously officers' property.

79. The column withdrew *via* Clary—Elincourt—Malincourt—Beaurevoir; reaching the last-named place between 8 and p.m. it halted there until midnight.

80. It may have been the detached Section of "D" R.H.A., about which nothing is known.

81. Lieut. E. L. Armitage, 27th Battery, R.F.A.

82. Probably the guns abandoned by 6 R.F.A. (*vide supra*.).

83. Probably the machine guns of the 2/R. Scots and 1/Gordon Highlanders 8th Infantry Brigade.

It is evident that in the centre of the line none of the difficulties were present that complicated the withdrawal of the Fifth Division from close contact with the foe. Between Troisvilles and Caudry the ground was far more favourable for defence and concealment; the batteries had made the most of the chance offered to them; and the bold use made of two advanced sections, dug in for the express purpose of close defence in the final stage, gave a result that equalled all expectations.[84]

(c.) Fourth Division.—(see map 4).

Just before 2 p.m. the German artillery opened a heavy fire on Haucourt and the ground to the south. Shortly afterwards XXIX was ordered to withdraw by batteries, and 127 and 126 succeeded in moving through this barrage with comparatively slight casualties.[85] The batteries fell back to a position in the Iris Valley between Caullery and Selvigny.

Probably about the same time XIV retired to a position immediately north of Selvigny.[86]

At 4 p.m. further arrangements were made in case it became necessary to withdraw from the position. It was now that 35 (Hows.) were ordered to move further back to a position behind the railway, so as to be able to cover the retirement of the rest of XXXVII. Whilst carrying out this move along the road to the south the battery was shelled and lost one man and one horse killed, as well as two men and several horses wounded, being forced also to abandon an ammunition wagon.[87] Meanwhile the other howitzer batteries—31 and 55—stood their ground and assisted to cover the retirement of XXXII.

About 5 p.m., most of the troops in front having fallen back, and being without any orders, Lieut.-Colonel Battiscombe, on his own

---

84. At 4 p.m. one of our observers saw that fires were burning in Caudry and that the German artillery were still shelling the place with considerable zeal. It was a compliment to the 7th Infantry Brigade. The same observer reported that he noticed some of the German Reserves disposed along the ridges to the north of the Le Cateau—Cambrai *chaussée*. It was too late now for their effective intervention, for the Second Corps had achieved its aim by sheer, hard fighting and the critical hour was just overpast.

85. 126 had 1 man wounded, 1 horse killed. 1 wagon destroyed; 127 had 5 men wounded, 10 horses killed, 2 wagons destroyed.

86. At 2.50 p.m. the Second Corps informed the Fourth Division that Corps H.Q. were leaving Bertry (G.391).

87. It is doubtful if this battery fired on August 26. It suffered more heavily than either of the other batteries in the brigade.

initiative, ordered 31 and 55 to limber up and retire. It was clear that the road used by 35 was registered, consequently the other two batteries were withdrawn through Selvigny. When quite clear the brigade commander halted them under cover and then rode off to find 35 and lead it back to the rest of the brigade.

At 4.30 p.m. the C.R.A. issued orders to the B.A.C's. that the Fourth Division was retiring *via* Selvigny—Malincourt—Villers Outréaux, and the columns, moving at once *via* Elincourt, were to join the main column at Walincourt.

The doings of XIV at the conclusion of this phase, in fact all day, are shrouded in obscurity. Had it not been for the sketch among the G.S. papers of the Fourth Division the various positions of the three batteries could not have been conjectured.

In XXIX, 125 was the last battery of its brigade to retire; it was the rearmost one of the three, being in action in the Iris valley to the west of Ligny. It limbered up under cover and then succeeded in getting across the 200 yards of open, immediately behind it, without suffering any casualties.

The real strain of saving their guns was reserved for 27 and 135 (both of XXXII). It will be recollected that 135 was in action, in dispersed sections, for close co-operation with the 11th Infantry Brigade in the defence of Ligny, to which the brigade had now fallen back. About 3.30. p.m. masses of German infantry showed up along the railway line, advancing in pursuit from Caudry and Beauvois. Fire was promptly opened on them and great execution was done. The battery remained in position ready for any target that offered, and by 5 p.m. most of our infantry had retired to Ligny; but 135 still held on to cover any further retirement. Any serious pressure must have caused the loss of the guns in their exposed position, but in this quarter the Germans had been taught a lesson and were very chary of closing as long as 135 was waiting to receive them.

Consequently it was decided to make an attempt to withdraw the guns, although orders to abandon them had been received from the B.G.C. 11th Infantry Brigade. Major Liveing decided that the guns could be saved, and the men hauled them out of action by hand so that they could be limbered up. Then as the situation did not appear critical the wagons were drawn back in a similar fashion, only one body being left behind.[88] By this time the Germans had dribbled

---

88. Fortunately an abandoned wagon was found on the southern outskirts of Ligny and this completed the equipment of the battery.

forward into dead ground, consequently two sections stood by with 80 shrapnel per gun, fuses set at "0", to deal with the last stage of the attack. Actually they were not wanted and the battery retired through Ligny, being the last unit to leave that place, and took the road to Caullery.[89]

The task performed by the senior battery in the brigade[90] was even more difficult than that of 135. The guns of 27 had been temporarily abandoned after the ammunition supply was exhausted, but the detachments remained under cover, close at hand, to withdraw them directly darkness fell. The C.R.A. himself saw the battery in action after the infantry had retired from its vicinity. Probably it was well after 5 p.m.[91] when, realising that Ligny must shortly be entered by the Germans, the brigade commander of XXXII called for volunteers from the battery to run out the guns by hand. The B.C., Major Vallentin, and the whole battery volunteered immediately. Men were then dribbled forward to the guns and, keeping under the cover of the shields, they set to work with picks and loosened the earth round the trails.

During pauses in the shelling a gun or a limber was run back to the road. Thus, by dint of steady work and seizing the opportunities offered, four guns and four limbers were withdrawn into the sunken road in rear. Then suddenly the firing increased and when the detachments were working on the next gun a heavy and accurate fire opened on the battery. A second attempt met with the same fate and most unwillingly it was decided that the enterprise must be abandoned, for its continuance might lead to its total failure. Forming up the four guns under cover they waited their time and then made a sudden dash to the south-westward, pursued by German shells—fortunately all were very short.[92] These four guns were saved.[93]

Whilst this phase of the action was in progress heavy firing was heard to the west. This proved to be the 75 mms. with General Sordet's

---

89. Le Cateau is the first war service recorded in the history of the battery. 135 (with 134) were formed at Sheffield in 1900. The author had the honour to be the first commanding officer of the former. Major Liveing was awarded the D.S.O. for his work with the battery on this day.

90. 27 was raised in 1794. In August 1913, 27 changed numbers, records, and services with 130 (vide Army Order 220 of 1913).

91. One account says it was at 5.30 p.m. that the battery received orders to retire.

92. The battery retired across country, N.C.O's having been sent on to cut the wire fences.

93. Major Vallentin was awarded the D.S.O., and the D.C.M. was given to 1 sergeants and 5 gunners.

Cavalry Corps coming into action and letting drive at any Germans that showed.[94] This reinforcement was most welcome and proved a sufficient deterrent on this flank.

It is clear that the pressure on the Fourth Division was far less severe than it had been on the Fifth Division. In fact, merely considering how the action ran its course to the west of Caudry, nothing had occurred in its own area to necessitate the withdrawal of the Fourth Division and, generally speaking, it got away without great difficulty and in fairly good formation.[95]

Consequently the withdrawal of the guns was achieved with hardly any serious loss, but this does not detract from the work of the officers and men of the two exposed batteries—27 and 135—who were determined to ensure that when their batteries retired they should do so as efficient fighting units.[96]

(d) Royal Horse Artillery.

It was about 3 p.m. that "E" and "L", in action astride the road north of Escaufort, opened on hostile columns advancing against the right flank and succeeded in arresting the movement. An hour later "L's" advanced section, which had been under very heavy fire, was successfully withdrawn, its retirement being covered by the fire of the other guns. The two batteries still maintained their position, for their orders were to remain in action until the Fifth Division had retired beyond Maretz. Only when the Roman Road between Reumont and Maretz was seen to be quite empty did the Batteries limber up and withdraw.[97] The cavalry and Horse Artillery retired at first on to the high ground to the east of the Honnechy—Busigny road; then at 7 p.m. the whole force drew off, moving *via* Busigny and Brancourt, to Ramicourt where it halted for the night.

---

94. Apparently General Sordet's French Cavalry Corps (presumably, I, III and V Cavalry Divisions), which had passed westward across the front of the battlefield on the previous evening, had taken up its position between Esnes and Lesdain covering the British left and it now came into action in the nick of time.

95. The 11th Infantry Brigade appears to have gone off as a formed body beyond Clary, so far as the men who were present were concerned. This also applies to the 12th Infantry Brigade.

96. Possibly it was as late as 4.30 p.m. when one of our observers saw a German infantry column, of about a regiment, moving south along the ridge near Wambaix with the obvious intention of outflanking the left of the Fourth Division. Once more it was too late; and any chance of gaining a crushing victory over the Second Corps on Aug. 20 had slipped for ever from the grasp of the German commander.

97. 5 p.m.? Assistance in fixing this time is required.

The I Cavalry Brigade had been with "E," and "L" all day. When the time came to withdraw, one gun of "L" was in so exposed a situation that its abandonment was discussed. But the B.G.C. I Cavalry Brigade decided that an attempt should be made to save it. Leading his brigade forward General Briggs reached the gun and brought it in. Only six days later, in the early dawn of Tuesday, September 1, at *Néry*, "L" repaid its obligation—when it stood by the I Cavalry Brigade to the death.

When the Fifth Division fell back the cavalry and its three Horse Artillery batteries, in *échelon* behind this flank, were well placed to prevent the German cavalry cutting in on the line of retreat down the Roman Road.

(E).—Covering Positions.

(a) Fifth Division.—(See map 5).

On reaching Reumont which was then on fire, one of the subalterns of 123 looked back over the position and saw masses of German infantry standing along the crest line, all leaning wearily on their rifles and pointing down the road to Reumont. "It might have been the end of a field day."

The left section of 61 (Hows.) came into action about 1000 yards behind the first position of the battery to cover the withdrawal of our Infantry and here it opened fire again on the German Infantry. The two howitzers remained in action until the B.C. was told that there were no formed bodies of our infantry between him and the enemy and he was then ordered to retire. Probably the battery was one of the last units in the Fifth Division to quit the field.

The single 60-pdr. of the first section of 108 Heavy Battery came into action again on the far side of Reumont to assist in covering the final withdrawal.[98] 80 R.F.A. also came into action about three miles south-west of Reumont to cover the retirement.

About 4.30 p.m. the gun limbers of 52 (of XV) were still waiting in a field between Reumont and Honnechy whilst a counter-attack was

---

98. It co-operated with the 1/Norfolk R. (15th Inf. Bde.) who were holding a. position east of Honnechy, covering the head of the long valley leading up from Lie Cateau. Fire was opened on a heavy German column (artillery and infantry) that was marching up the valley road. The 60-pdr., having no shrapnel left, loosed off lyddite at the column. This and the long-range rifle fire of the 1/Nor. R. was sufficient and the threatening advance died out at once. It was shortly after 4.30 p.m. This column was seen by one of our air observers at 1 p.m. issuing from Le Cateau. He considered it was a German regiment.

contemplated for the recapture of the abandoned guns.[99] It was decided however not to deliver this stroke, and the limbers then joined in the retirement down the Roman Road.[100]

Perhaps the finest example of discipline in this phase was given by 122. The two guns that had been saved and two ammunition wagons[101] were collected out of a mass of riderless horses and scattered vehicles, and the B.C.—Major Sanders—and a subaltern at once went into action with them to cover the withdrawal. A rearguard was then forming in front of Maurois and Honnechy and 122 came into action to the south-west of the latter place. After some time (the B.C. thought about 6 p.m.) a German column was seen marching up the valley road. The two guns at once opened fire. After a dozen rounds the column disappeared and did not show up again.

Oh this flank only had the Germans succeeded in gaining anything approaching a success,[102] after massing probably two corps against one division. Left in possession of this part of the field, as they were, they evinced no passionate desire to open an immediate and relentless pursuit, such as their forbears had started after their victory at Leuthen, or after Waterloo—in each of which battles their adversaries may have been fitly termed "overwhelmed".

On the 26th August 1914 the most powerful and best equipped fighting machine ever put into the field up to that time, flushed too with the joy of a campaign successfully opened, had been opposed in a bitter fight by a force of half its strength that stood undauntedly at bay to bar its further onrush. By the end of that day the attackers had been beaten to a standstill, and so mauled that their only desire was to allow the Second Corps to continue its withdrawal from the field unmolested, save by the sullen boom of the German guns; and their

99. This is the most eloquent testimony to the spirit of the troops at the time of the retirement on the exposed right flank. The Second Corps was not overwhelmed at Le Cateau.

100. In XV R.F.A.. out of eighteen officers, only four (one captain and three subalterns) remained unwounded at the close of the action The command of XV now devolved on Captain A. B. Higgon of 80 R.F.A. Heavy casualties of this description should be remembered when studying the advance to the Aisne.

101. One belonged to 52 R.F.A.

102. 27 guns, out of the 36 that were lost, were abandoned on this flank. The losses suffered in guns by the other two divisions dispose once and for all of the theory that they were "overwhelmed." Even on the right flank some of the last units to leave the field marched away in fours from Reumont down the Roman Road, notably the 1/Queen's Own, Royal West Kent Regiment and a party of the 2/A. & S. Highlanders.

unsupported fire at this moment was the sure proof of the discomfiture suffered by the German host.

For four days the pressure and pursuit had been those of an army, a conquering army. But the action of Le Cateau fought on Wednesday, 26th August, 1914, changed the character of the pursuit of the German Army and thereafter it degenerated into a respectful pursuit by mounted troops and mobile detachments only. When it marched forward from the Le Cateau battlefield the German I Army continued its south-westerly advance until it was over the Somme; whereas, after the action, the line of withdrawal of the Second Corps was practically due South. On August 31 von Kluck changed the direction of his march and headed in a south-easterly direction. He now desired to cut off the Vth French Army, which had turned about and fought at Guise against the German II Army.

On September 1, in this rush to the south-east, he brushed against the B.E.F. at Néry, Crépy en Valois, and Villers Cotterèts (south and south-east of Compiegne). To this respite the artillery of the Fifth Division had contributed in a very marked degree.

(b) Third Division—(See map 5).

In this section there was little or no real pursuit About 3.30 p.m., XXIII (in conjunction with the 9th Infantry Brigade) took up a covering position from Bertry to Montigny, about 2000 yards behind their first position, and at once ranged on the line previously occupied by the infantry so as to be ready to deal immediately with any serious advance. No enemy were visible and after waiting about half an hour the retirement was resumed.[103]

29 (of XLII) also took up a covering position near Clary; but no targets presented themselves and after remaining in action for some time the march southward was continued.

There is no doubt that no attempt was made by the Germans to press on in the centre when the Third Division fell back. The position was naturally a strong one and it had been most skilfully occupied. Any desire the Germans may have possessed to keep touch with the Third Division was roughly opposed by the guns of the two advanced sections of 107 and 108 which blew away the attacking troops as they shewed, and subdued any desire to press on. The 1/Gordon Highland-

---

103. The 9th Infantry Brigade did not pass through Clary till 6.30 p.m. They were marching as a formed body and they had moved in the same way from Troisvilles, when they retired from the original position to the covering one east of Montigny. In the centre the situation was well in hand.

ers (8th Infantry Brigade) and Companies of the 2/Royal Scots and 2/Royal Irish Regiment maintained their original position between Audencourt and Caudry until nearly midnight, the Germans making no attempt to close with them.[104]

(c) Fourth Division.—(See map 5).

To cover the retirement from Ligny, 127 (of XXIX) came into action about half a mile south of the village, and it was decided if necessary to face the loss of the Battery in order to ensure withdrawing the 11th Infantry Brigade clear of the place. Actually the Germans did not press on, consequently the Battery was not called upon to make the supreme sacrifice and as soon as the situation permitted it was safely withdrawn.

126, of the same brigade, was also brought into action to assist in covering the further retirement.[105]

A final position was taken up about 1 mile to the south-south-east of Selvigny, in conjunction with the Composite Regiment of Household Cavalry,[106] to cover the formation of the marching column.

Thus, broadly speaking, the artillery occupied one covering position after another, the batteries passing through each other in turn. But the Germans never attempted any pursuit at all[107] and the column retired unmolested from the field, marching *via* Villers Outréaux. [108]

The one outstanding fact is that the retirement on the left flank was carried out far later than it was either on the right or in the centre—convincing proof that the Germans did not appreciate the importance of this wing.

One of our airmen, flying over the field about 5 p.m., could see no infantry engaged, but he noticed that there was "considerable gunfire, chiefly German." In support of this statement it is recorded that after the Fourth Division had withdrawn from its positions the German artillery behaved here as it did all along the line. With Prussian thoroughness it subjected our vacated trenches and gun positions to a heavy bombardment—entirely satisfactory from our point of view. It

---

104. The order to retire did not reach these units.

105. Some of our infantry were in Haucourt until after dark.

106. They had also co-operated with 127 to the south of Ligny.

107. German infantry were not seen again by the infantry of the Fourth Division until September 1 at Verberie—south of the Forest of Compiegne.

108. The Fourth D.A.C. detrained at S. Quentin between 11 p.m., 25 Aug., and about noon, 26 Aug. As it arrived the column formed up on the road, and at 3.30 p.m. it marched to Ham on the Somme, arriving there at 9 p.m.

wasted a considerable amount of valuable time as well as a great deal of ammunition. This exhibition of misdirected energy was clear proof of the heavy nature of the German casualties at Le Cateau and the serious need for reorganisation in their army before any vigorous pursuit could be undertaken. The Second Corps had not fought in vain.

(d) Royal Horse Artillery.—(See map 4 & 5)

"I" R.H.A., still in action to the west of Montigny, received orders at 3 p.m. to join the IV Cavalry Brigade to the south of Ligny. The cavalry brigade and the battery were then ordered to take up a position to prevent the Germans debouching from the large woods south of Walincourt and thus cover the retirement of the Fourth Division from the field.

"I" and the IV Cavalry Brigade remained in this position from 6 p.m. until dark, but the enemy never appeared and "I" then moved to Le Catelet.[109]

---

109. On Aug. 27, "I" was engaged with German infantry in the neighbourhood of Vendhuille. Later that afternoon (about 4 p.m.) German infantry columns (with transport) were seen marching towards Péronne

CHAPTER 9

The Retreat on St. Quentin

(See map 1).

At 3.30 p.m. G.H.Q. of the B.E.F. moved from S. Quentin to Noyon, which was reached at 5 p.m. At 1 a.m. General Sir Horace Smith-Dorrien arrived to report the day's proceedings to the commander-in-chief. He was able to inform Sir John French that although the men were very tired and wanted food yet he hoped to reform when daylight came. (Commander-in Chief's Diary.). Long as the day had been for the troops it was no shorter or less trying for the commander of the Second Corps, who only left G.H.Q., at Noyon. at 3 a.m. to return to S. Quentin, where he would then at once have to face the work of re-forming his corps.

The Divisional lines of retirement were broadly as follows.—
Fifth Division—along the Roman Road *via* Estrées (where there was a halt of some hours), to St. Quentin.

Third Division—*via* Elincourt, Beaurevoir, Hargicourt, keeping to the northward of the Roman Road.

Fourth Division—through Selvigny, Malincourt, Villers Outréaux, in other words along roads to the northward again of those used by the Third Division.

There is no doubt that some writers have exaggerated the scene, during the first stage of the retreat, into a mere panic rout. Nothing could be further from the truth.[1] The strain was bound to be felt most along the Roman Road. All those bodies of troops which retired

---

1. The evidence of one of our air-observers is very much to the point, reporting what he saw about 5 p.m., stated, "The British retirement appeared general, but orderly."

along the other roads, to northward, although they were considerably mixed up yet they marched in formation and were definitely under control.

Along the Roman Road this was not the case. Down that *Via Dolorosa* swirled a rudderless horde of men, guns, wagons, limbers without guns, carts, riderless horses. As units came into this stream they were engulfed in it, formations being broken up and cohesion lost. With nightfall it became harder to move and numerous long checks took place. Rain began to fall. The misery of hunger, thirst, and extreme fatigue could hardly be borne. Yet these men were soldiers still. Wounded and exhausted men were assisted along by their comrades, others were carried on wagons, guns, limbers, and carts. All kept their rifles and ammunition; for none had abandoned themselves to despair. In fact it was not a rout or panic, merely extreme confusion. Naturally no one who took part in it could ever forget that Wednesday night.

Physical and mental weariness were alone enough to have put the finishing touch to any other army the world has ever seen. Yet these worn out, footsore officers and men, who had fought and marched and fought again since Sunday morning, trudged on along a dreary road that must have seemed to all like one of those interminable ways in Hell that Dante has described, sustained only by the knowledge that it was their duty to keep moving until they could be organised once more in their old historic units.

Gradually with the dawn the staff began to straighten out this throng of men. By the time St. Quentin was finally passed units had been collected, (see note following), columns had been reformed, the men had had some food, and they had begun to realise the price the Germans had paid for attempting to attack them; their spirits were rising. The tide had turned at last, and although the time to advance was not yet, yet the way was being prepared for it. For the price of ultimate victory had been paid on Wednesday at Le Cateau by these gallant officers and men of the Second Corps.

Note:—The following marching details may be interesting:—
Between August 24 and 25, when it detrained in the neighbourhood of Le Cateau, until it reached Brie Comte Robert, south-east of Paris on September 5, at the end of the retirement, the Fourth Division marched 151½ miles in 11 marching days.
From 22—28 Aug. (7 days) 61 (Hows.) marched 110 miles, the

horses being without, or on short rations.

Between 20—28 Aug. (9 days) 108 Heavy Battery had marched 126 miles, a most creditable performance.

On 31 Aug. 52 R.F.A. formed 20 mounted rifles. The morale of the battery was as good as ever.

It was on 29 Aug. that the diary of XXXVII (Hows.), IV Division, was able to record, "Troops all in good health and spirits." The Germans were now to realise the truth of Napoleon's sage remark, "*Profitez des faveurs de la fortune lorsque ses caprices sont pour vous; elle est femme.*"

A forced march by a battery that may be recalled was that of 62 R.F.A. (less one section) under Major Granet, from Orange River Bridge to the Modder River Battlefield in 1899. Starting at 10 a.m., on 27 Nov., 62 reached the field at 2 p.m. on 28 Nov. In twenty-eight hours the battery had covered 62 miles. Six horses fell dead in the traces and forty more never recovered from their exhaustion. By 2.45 p.m. the battery was engaging the Boers along the north bank of the river and when the day closed had expended nearly 250 rounds. (*Official History of the War in South Africa*, Vol. I.).

CHAPTER 10

Comments on the Action

For the gunner and the student the handling of the artillery of the Second Corps in the action of Le Cateau will always possess an interest entirely its own. The action was fought by the regiment as we all knew it, by brigades and batteries with the old familiar numbers and letters, by units trained in peace by those officers who then commanded them m the field. The training of the officers themselves was based on the doctrines emphasized in our training manuals—teaching that was now to be put into practice against the most powerful, the best armed, and the best found army in the world. This army for nearly half a century had been crowned with a legend of invincibility, a fiction implicitly believed in by itself and one to which nearly all the rest of the world subscribed. It was a myth for ever dissipated in smoke at Le Cateau, after it had been blown to shreds from the lean mouths of our guns. Thus, on the Allied side, Le Cateau possesses a first-rate importance, for it is the first milestone on the long road to ultimate victory.

A.—General Comments.

Considering their crushing numerical superiority, their great preponderance in guns and machine guns, and the quantity of ammunition they expended, the amount of success achieved by the Germans in the action of Le Cateau was astonishingly small.

On Wednesday morning, August 26, the Germans possessed every conceivable advantage, in information, situation, numbers, and armament. Through their superior air-service[1] they must have known, or ought to have known, the bivouacking areas of the First Corps and

---

1. In August, 1914, their supremacy in this respect was due to their superior preparedness.

also of those units of the Second Corps that reached their halting places before dark.

Further confirmation about the First Corps was obtained from the fighting on Tuesday evening at Landrécies and Maroilles. The moves of the First Corps early on Wednesday could be kept under observation from the air. Given such a situation at the opening of one of Napoleon's great campaigns, it would be an interesting speculation to consider what profit he would have derived from it. At the end of the 26th it is certain that he would have been able to claim something more tangible as a success than having allowed the First Corps to escape, together with the barren honour of having gained a Pyrrhic victory at Le Cateau. He would have achieved more than the mere occupation of the battlefield when the heavily outnumbered British Force had relinquished it, after having beaten their numerically superior assailants to a standstill in a fierce and bitter fight for the less essential part of the position.

It has been suggested that the exposure of the batteries of XV and XXVIII R.F.A. was the primary cause that tempted the Germans to mass against the right flank of the Second Corps and led them to anticipate an easy success at that end of the battle line. If this is ever proved to be the case then the loss suffered by these gallant brigades in their forward positions will be far more than justified.[2] For there can be no doubt that the first of the two principal mistakes made by the German command on this day was its decision to concentrate its great effort against the British right in the neighbourhood of Le Cateau.

The second undoubtedly was the German failure to open an immediate and relentless pursuit directly the Fifth Division commenced its retirement. Judged by the supreme test, of being able to reap all the advantages of the success he had then won, it is clear that the German commander at Le Cateau was merely *un bon général ordinaire* for he failed to exhibit real driving energy at that hour. He allowed the weariness of his troops, the heavy losses they had suffered, the ammunition they had expended to weigh him down and render him immobile . Thus the golden hours of opportunity passed by whilst he

2. Had the Second Corps continued its retirement voluntarily or been driven back on S. Quentin early on Aug. 26 the Germans would have had a splendid opportunity to crush the First Corps on that day. This may explain the concentration of the German strength against the right of the Fifth Division. Here around Le Cateau the overwhelming hostile force was fully employed by the Second Corps during the critical hours of Aug. 26 and the First Corps crossed the Sambre without undue difficulty.

was engaged in the profitless task of digesting his joy over his barren victory.

To return to the first of these two mistakes. It is quite clear, when the situation is studied, that the left (or west) was the vital flank. To crush in the centre must take too long and prove far too costly. To drive in the right flank could lead to nothing decisive unless it was followed up immediately and vigorously. Directly the Germans were content to employ an infantry sickle to reap what was merely left lying on the field itself, instead of using a cavalry scythe to cut down the real harvest that remained, then it was certain that the Second Corps would soon shake itself together and regain its morale for more than two-thirds of it had none the worse of the day's fighting. The retirement would be carried out along the roads still left open, the operations of the two British corps would once more be combined, and the most effective co-operation arranged between the B.E.F. and the armies of our gallant Ally.

Actually whilst enveloping the right flank of the Second Corps the Germans, tempted by their numerical superiority and the success hitherto achieved, made a very feeble attempt to envelop the left; but in face of the unshaken defence of that flank, and the presence of General Sordet's Cavalry beyond it, the attempt was not pressed. Yet had they been content with a simple manoeuvre and contained the right and centre, whilst as early as possible throwing overwhelming strength against our left flank, then they might have achieved a great result.[3]

Our troops were later on the ground here than was the case with the heads of the other divisions, the artillery was all in Ligny, the ground apparently had not been reconnoitred, and no positions had been prepared so far to the west of Le Cateau. On the other hand this section of the line is no further from Bavai than is the right flank.[4]

---

3. So far as can be ascertained at present, the original frontal attack was made by two corps and a cavalry division—the IV and IV (Reserve) Corps and the 9th Cavalry Division. The IV German Corps attacked from Le Cateau and the Selle Valley (exclusive) to about Troisvilles and Audencourt; whilst the IV (Reserve) Corps frontage was from about Audencourt to Esnes, the 9th German Cavalry Division probably beginning the attack in front of Haucourt against the 12th Infantry Brigade. Later the III Corps advanced through Le Cateau and up the Selle Valley against the British right, whilst the II Corps was available to use against our left. The 4th Cavalry Division may have remained in reserve all day, as it had fought a fairly severe action, overnight, at Solesmes.

4. The extreme left of the line, the village of Esnes, was held all day (till about 4.30 p.m.) by 2 Companies and 2 machine guns of the 2/Royal Inniskilling Fusiliers.

Once the left flank was driven in the whole retreat of the B.E.F. must have been endangered. The Roman Road must have become much more congested, for the Fourth Division would have been forced back on to the Third and the two together, if the Germans followed up at all, would have been driven across the line of retirement of the Fifth Division, which would probably have had to hold on to let the others open their retirement on St. Quentin.

Had the advantage then been pressed the whole of the Second Corps might have been shouldered off towards Guise, blocking the only lines of withdrawal open to the First Corps. An irretrievable disaster would then have taken place. The only alternative open to the Second Corps would have been to stand its ground fighting to the last, and thus ensure at any rate the safe withdrawal of the First Corps. Even this alternative had been faced by Sir H. Smith-Dorrien in the early hours of that Wednesday. Confident of himself, he had also implicit confidence in his men. He knew that on August 26, whichever way the battle might turn, the Second Corps would put up "a real grand fight." It will give the deepest satisfaction to all future historians to record that his confidence was amply justified; and both his generalship and his character rose far superior to the critical occasion.[5] For on that August day, as the fierce fight swayed and surged, he remained the master—both of himself and of the situation—and in his eager grip the sword bit deep into the German host.

The commander in chief, Field Marshal Sir John French, was the first to recognise what the commander of the Second Corps had done on August 26; and he did so in words that will stand so long as an account of this war is read:—[6]

> . . . . .I cannot close the brief account of this glorious stand of the British troops without putting on record my deep appreciation of the valuable services rendered by General Sir Horace Smith Dorrien.
>
> I say without hesitation that the saving of the left wing of the army under my command on the morning of August 26 could never have been accomplished unless a commander of rare

5. "*Il faut qu'un homme de guerre ait autant de caractère que d'esprit. Les hommes qui ont beaucoup d'esprit et peu de caractère y sont les moins propres; c'est un navire qui a une mâture disproportionnée à son lest; il vaut mieux beaucoup de caractère et peu d'esprit. Les hommes qui ont médiocrement d'esprit et un caractère proportionné réussiront souvent dans ce métier; il faut autant de base que de hauteur.*" (Napoléon.).

6. Despatch, dated 7 Septr., 1911.

and unusual coolness, intrepidity, and determination had been present to conduct the operation personally.

(B).—TACTICAL COMMENTS.

It is time to turn to the consideration of the handling of the troops and particularly of the artillery in this action. It is obvious that it is still too near the event for any full criticism of the details of the action. At the present time we are only beginning to learn what actually occurred; consequently it is necessary, at this stage, to appreciate what was done, leaving till a much later date any attempt to draw all possible lessons from this battle. For our present purpose it is wise to recall the teaching of our training manuals anent a delaying action.

Field Service Regulations, Part 1, deals with a delaying action in Chapter 7, para. 114. It states clearly that:

> The delaying power of a numerically inferior force is greatly affected by the ground . . . . . The guiding principle in all delaying action must be that when an enemy has liberty to manoeuvre the passive occupation of a position, however strong, can rarely be justified, and always involves the risk of crushing defeat; under these circumstances a delaying force must manoeuvre so as to force an enemy to deploy as often as possible, but should rarely accept battle

A consideration of the situation and the condition of the Second Corps, on Wednesday morning must convince anyone that, if it was to avoid disaster, it was bound to accept battle in the Le Cateau position, and that this is one of those rare occurrences when the only means of gaining sufficient time was by engaging the enemy, the G.O.C. being ready to break off the fight directly the necessary time was gained. The passive occupation of the position beyond that hour would lead to the isolation of the Second Corps by the I German Army, for the latter possessed full liberty of manoeuvre on that day. The risk was great. The responsibility resting on the shoulders of the Commander of the Second Corps was heavy. Fortunately the execution was equal to the conception and thus the desired end was attained.

Field Service Regulations, Part 1, Chapter 5, para. 72, deals with the handling of a rear guard, and much of this teaching applies to the dispositions of the delaying force at Le Cateau. It lays stress on:

> Showing as strong a front to the enemy as possible, and making sure of good lines of retreat.

The greater part of the force should be in the fighting line from the outset . . . . as great a display of force as possible being made.

Both these points are admirably illustrated by the position selected and the skilful arrangements made of the available troops. The length of the position occupied by the Second Corps on August 26 was virtually 13 miles. To hold this there were available about 32,000 bayonets (allowing for the losses of 23-25 August)[7] which gives rather less than 1.5 men per yard of front, a suitable proportion for a delaying action.

The question of reserves is also well illustrated. Practically all the spare troops, available as a General Reserve, were the rather scattered cavalry division and the 19th Infantry Brigade, a by no means excessive amount considering the length of the position, the open nature of both flanks, and the preponderating amount of artillery that the enemy could unlimber.

The Germans fully realise that no decisive victory can be gained without suffering bloody losses; or as one of their writers says:

When necessary, to sacrifice ruthlessly the life of the soldier in battle is the great law of war, to which both the soldier and the officer must conform with equal readiness.

Consequently it is remarkable that no resolute and sustained effort was made to destroy the Second Corps on August 26. Had a determined assault been delivered all along the line, between 1 and 2 p.m., the Second Corps would have been forced to fight it out just where it stood; and the arrival of fresh troops on the German side would have enabled the assailants to deliver a death-blow to the hopelessly outnumbered defenders. No trace exists of such an attack; the will to conquer was absent. The German leaders felt their way cautiously, weighed the *pros* and *cons*, and waited; they let go their hold upon the Second Corps and the precious moment slipped away, never to return. Such is war!

Another "point of great importance to the commander is to judge accurately the time to retire." On August 26 it was essential to gain every possible moment and yet, if possible, to break off the action before the Germans definitely gained the upper hand on the left flank. As the action ran there was no great risk of the latter event occurring,

---

7. See Note to Appendix 3.

and everything actually turned on how long the right flank could withstand the pounding to which it was subjected. No unit on that right flank has any cause to recall the Action of Le Cateau with anything but extreme pride. The troops on the right of the Fifth Division were fought out to the last limits of their human endurance, and when the G.O.C., who had kept his hand on the pulse of the fight, was finally compelled to sanction the retirement he had gained sufficient time. But his nerve had never failed him for he had not broken off the action a moment too soon.

With special reference to the artillery the manual states:—

The artillery shall be able to open fire on the attacking artillery at a long range and compel his infantry to deploy at the greatest possible distance.

This was extremely difficult to apply on the ground, because of the misty light in the early morning, the undulating nature of the country, and the covered approaches through the existing valleys. However sufficient range was obtainable to bring up the German infantry attacks all standing, wherever our guns had not been silenced previously by an overwhelming fire.

The next principle enunciated is that "the artillery should cover the withdrawal of the infantry." This was done by 61 (Hows.), 108 Heavy Battery, and the remaining section of 122 in the Fifth Division; by the brusque reception given to the attacking infantry in the centre by the advanced sections of 107 and 108 R.F.A., in the Third Division; and was due to the fire of 135 R.F.A. in the Fourth Division, and the readiness to sacrifice 127 to cover the evacuation of Ligny.

Further "it should be possible to withdraw the artillery without difficulty." Except in the cases of XV R.F.A. and 37 (Hows.) closely supporting the 2/Suffolk Regiment (14th Infantry Brigade), XXVIII R.F.A. carrying out the same duty for 2/K.O.Y.L.I, and 2/K.O.S.B. (13th Infantry Brigade) in the Fifth Division; the case of the two advanced sections of 107 and 108 in the Third Division, deliberately placed to afford the closest co-operation to their infantry at a crisis; and the case of 135 and 127 in the Fourth Division, closely engaged for the same reason, all the artillery was so placed that withdrawal was not unduly difficult. Further, in each division the artillery was echeloned in depth and, when the Germans occupied the original positions, every discouragement to press on was offered by batteries already in action in rear and registered on the old line.

Our own manual, *Field Artillery Training*, deals with the *Employment of Artillery in War* in chapter 7, and rearguard work is considered in Sections 165 and 166. It lays down:

> When it is a question of ensuring the safe withdrawal of the main body, artillery must be ready to take any risk, and loss of materiel is then fully justified.

The artillery of the Second Corps obeyed this teaching in the letter as well as in the spirit on August 26.

Further in Section 165 it says that:

> Should it become necessary to abandon a position, a portion of the artillery will be required to establish itself as quickly as possible in positions from which the retirement of the rest of the force can be covered. The fire of heavy guns from positions overlooking the main position, combined with that of field guns which, owing to their greater mobility, may occupy more advanced positions, would usually form the most effective means for securing the withdrawal of the rest of the force . . . .

The disposition of the heavy guns naturally applies chiefly to the artillery in the Fifth Divisional Area, and there is no doubt that it is exemplified perfectly by the positions occupied by 61 (Hows.) and 108 Heavy Battery. Both batteries were able to retain their original retired positions, when the front line of their division fell back, and the barrage they put down at once, on to the old position, acted as a great deterrent to any immediate pursuit beyond it.

Our manual also states that:

> A rearguard is usually strong in artillery . . . . positions in rear of a crest are preferable . . . the flanks of a rearguard position are specially important and some guns should usually be employed in their defence.

Here, at Le Cateau, all the artillery was deployed for the delaying action that was to be fought. In the case of XV R.F.A. and 37 (Hows.), on the right flank of the Fifth Division, it may be considered that it would have been wiser to place only sections in the forward position, the rest of the guns being brought into action in the valley and about three-quarters of a mile further back. Had this course been pursued a more difficult target would have been presented to the German artillery in the misty light of the early morning; the batteries would have been less liable to be doubly enfiladed; the spur south of Le Cateau could have been kept under effective fire; the southern exits from the town, as well as the Selle valley, could have been denied to the German infantry; and nearly all the guns could have been saved.

On the other hand it must not be forgotten that the position was clearly indicated to the brigade commander by the C.R.A. of the division; it was taken up in order to afford, their Infantry, continual and close support in a fight to a finish; and the First Corps was expected to cover and secure its right flank. Neither must it be overlooked that there had been no time to make any adequate reconnaissance of the ground; nor was their any idea, on the right flank, that the action to be fought was really to be one of a delaying character.

In order to appreciate the dispositions suggested by *Field Artillery Training* the arrangement of the batteries of the Third Division should be studied closely. Here the ground was eminently suitable. Certainly no flank was involved, otherwise the arrangements are strictly in accord with the advice of the training manual, with the one addition that makes them so admirable an illustration of the broad spirit in which text books should be read and applied—the use of the two advanced sections to give the necessary close co-operation with the Infantry at the crisis. This proves that the duty of training manuals is to assist and train common-sense; they cannot take its place. Talent cannot be replaced by a regulation.

That the help thus afforded by the artillery at Le Cateau was appreciated, by their comrades of the infantry, was touchingly shown next morning. Exhausted as they were by the long night march, yet many men stepped out of the ranks as they passed to give a silent pat to the guns drawn up by the roadside.[8]

Thus it is clear that the delaying action fought by the Second Corps at Le Cateau is a teaching example which will well repay the diligent study of all gunners.

Whereas in the actions fought in the neighbourhood of Mons, on August 23 and 24, the heavy German casualties could be largely put down to the rapid fire of our infantry,[9] at Le Cateau there can be no doubt that the very severe losses suffered by the Germans were mainly the result of our gun fire. Both the tactical handling of the artillery and

---

8. Extract from the diary of the C.R.A., Fifth Division.

9. An exception must be made of the Flank Guard action at Audregnies on August 24. Here the damage and stopping effect were due largely to the fire of the four batteries engaged—"L," "D," "E," R.H.A. and 119 R.F.A.

the technical training of the personnel had been justly appreciated and developed on sound lines. When the chance was offered each commander was ready to use his battery as a single six-barrelled weapon with which he hit, at exactly the right moment and with crushing effect.

The noble and stately motto of "*Ubique*" is honoured by the inclusion of Le Cateau among the services that it commemorates. For a ray of glory shone on those batteries that thundered forth defiance to the foe on that field in Cambrésis over four long years ago, (as at time of first publication).

Appendix 1

Copy of O.O. 2, Fourth Division.[1]

10th, 11th, 12th Bdes.   O.O. 2.
Div. Art.

As originally arranged (see O.O. No. 1) the Expeditionary Force will take up a position on approx. line Le Cateau—Carrières[2]—Mont d'Esnes.[3] (approxy).

Disposition IV Div.—Le Coquelet Fme.—Mont d'Esnes.[3]

XI Bde will occupy position from Le Coquelet Fme.[4] to Rly.[5] about South of O of Fontaine.[6]

XII Bde will occupy position from Rly. about South of O of Fontaine,[7] to Mont d'Esnes,[3] just N.W. of Esnes.

X Bde. Haucourt (Reserve).

All these under G.O.C. R.A.:—

14 and 29 F.A. Bdes. East of Esnes
32 and 37 F.A. Bdes. at Ligny

Div. H.Q. remain at Haucourt.

These positions to be taken up at once and entrenched as strongly as possible.   (sd) J. E. Edmonds, Col., G.S. IV Div.[8]
Haucourt, 26/8/14, 6 a.m.

---

1. Copies are to be found among the Appendices to Vol. 1. of G. S. Diary, Fourth Division, and also attached to Vol. I. of C.R.A.'s Diary, Fourth Division.

2. "Serainvillers" has been erased.

3. Moulin d'Esnes is meant.

4. "About U of CAUDRY" has been erased.

5. "Stn" has been erased.

6. "Cattenières (incl.)" has been erased.

7. Rly. Stn. S. of Cattenières" has been erased. All the corrections are written above the erased words.

8. On the copy among the appendices to the G. S. Diary is written in pencil—"Some of these readied units, some did not."

Appendix 2

GUNS LOST BY R.A., SECOND CORPS, AT LE CATEAU
ON 26 AUGUST 1914.

Fifth Division.

XV R.F.A:

11 R.F.A.	2
80 R.F.A.	1
37/VIII (Hows.) R.F.A.	1
52 R.F.A.	6

XXVIII R.F.A.

122 R.F.A..	4
123 R.F.A.	6
124 R.F.A.	6
108 Heavy Battery, R.G.A. (upset in ditch)	1
	—
	27

Third Division.

XXIII R.F.A.

107 R.F.A. (advanced section)	2
108 R.F.A. (advanced section)	2
XL R.F.A. 6R.F.A	3
	—
	7

Fourth Division.

XXXII R.F.A. 27 R.F.A	2
	—
	2
	—
Grand Total	= 36

Total—34, 18 pdrs.
1, 4. 5" howitzer.
1, 60 pdr.

There also appear to have been about 15 limbers and 50 ammunition wagons left on the field in the Fifth Divisional Area.

Appendix 3

Royal Artillery Casualties on 26 August, 1914.

The records are most meagre in the diaries and require supplementing. The only recorded losses are as follows:—

Fifth Division.—

XV

H.Q. Staff 1 officer missing (Brigade Major)

Brigade Staff 3 officers wounded and missing, 16 other ranks casualties.

14 officer killed, 4 wounded, 36 other ranks casualties; and 58 horses.[1]

52 1 officer wounded, 2 wounded and missing. Other ranks 3 killed, 23 wounded, 8 missing; 102 horses.[1]

80 1 officer killed, 1 wounded, 1 missing; 38 other ranks casualties; 70 horses.[1]

At least 44 officers, 124 other ranks; and 230 horses.

XXVIII

Brigade Staff 1 officer killed.

122 1 officer killed, 1 officer wounded, at least 8 other ranks killed, 14 wounded; 20 horses.

123 2 officers wounded; other ranks 5 killed, 18 wounded.

124 1 officer killed; 13 other ranks casualties.

At least 6 officers, 58 other ranks; and 20 horses.

XXVII None recorded.

VIII (Hows)

37 (Hows.). 1 officer wounded and missing.

65 (Hows.). 2 other ranks wounded; 7 horses

---

1. The numbers of the horse casualties in XV are based on those given in the C.R.A.'s Diary.

108 Heavy Battery No record.

Ammunition Columns No record.

Total Artillery casualties Fifth Division, so far as recorded:—
22 officers, 180 other ranks, 257 horses.

Third Division:—

XXIII

108 3 other ranks missing (patrol; 1 horse wounded.
109 4 horses.

The above are the only casualties recorded in the R.A. Diaries,
Third Division.

Fourth Division:—

XXXII

27 1 Officer wounded; other ranks, 1 killed, 7 wounded.

XXIX

126 1 wounded; 1 horse killed.
127 5 wounded; 10 horses killed.

XIV

88 1 Officer killed.

XXXVII

31 1 wounded; some horses.
35 1 killed, 2 wounded; 1 horse killed,, several wounded.

The recorded casualties in the Fourth Division amount to:—
2 officers, 18 other ranks, 12 horses.

R.HA.

No casualties are recorded in the R.H.A. Diaries.

The total recorded casualties for the R.A. at Le Cateau amount
to:—
24 officers, 201 other ranks, 274 horses.

More information on this point is required.

Note.[2]

The infantry of the Fifth Division, which had numbered 12,000
and 24 machine guns on August 22, probably lost 2,300 up to
and including August 25, as well as some machine guns destroyed by gunfire.

---

2. I am entirely indebted to Capt. Atkinson for the figures given in this note, they
are based on the evidence of the diaries, few of which give detailed statements.

Note:—The losses then fell somewhat as follows:—

13th Infantry Brigade	900
14th " "	400
15th " "	1,000

By Aug. 29, 18 of the 24 m. guns were reported lost or destroyed.

These losses must be borne in mind when the advance from the Seine to the Aisne is being considered. To talk of a brigade then and imagine it as still consisting of 4,000 rifles and 3 machine guns is extremely misleading.

To take two examples from the artillery of the Fifth Division:— XV R.F.A., after Le Cateau, had 9, instead of 18, 18 pdrs.; whilst XXVIII R.F.A. had only 2 18 pdrs. until after the Aisne was crossed.

Thus at Le Cateau the Fifth Division was not more than 9,700 infantry. The approximate losses it suffered on this day were as follows:—

Fifth Division:—

14th Infantry Brigade	1,250
13th " "	950
15th " "	150
	———
Total =	2,350

This loss is about 25% of the infantry engaged.
The other losses along the line were broadly as follows:—

Third Division:—

9th Infantry Brigade	150
8th " "	1,000[3]
7th " "	300
	———
Total =	1,450

This loss is about 15% of the infantry engaged.[4]

Fourth Division:—

11th Infantry Brigade	1,150

3. Of the losses shown for the 8th Infantry Brigade about three-quarters were due to the fact that, owing to an accident, the 1/Gordon Highlanders and flanking companies did not receive orders to retire (see chapter 8).

4. A message sent, on August 26, by the Second Corps to the Fifth Division, ran:— "Third Division about 2,000 below normal strength, and full of fight."

12th	"	"	1,000
10th	"	"	1,000
	Total	=	3,150

This loss is rather more than 25% of the infantry engaged. [5]

19th Infantry Brigade (reserve)   550.

This makes the total infantry loss about 7,500.

Consequently the total loss at Le Cateau will not exceed 8,000 men out of a total of 50,000 engaged, and does not substantiate the theory that the force was overwhelmed.

Also between 2,500 and 3,000 men, footsore and exhausted, were despatched by rail to the advanced base at Le Mans for recuperation and refitting. They must therefore be deducted from the available fighting strength on August 28, when General Sir Horace Smith-Dorrien's force had taken up a position on the Oise.

5. The units of the Fourth Division were practically at full strength on Aug. 26.

Appendix 4

The records are pitiably insufficient in this particular. All that is given is as follows:—

Fifth Division:—

XV

80 (6 wagons at least)	456 lost 1 gun
52 (about)	1,100[1] lost 6 guns

XXVIII

122 (about)	600 lost 4 guns
123 (6 wagons at least)	456 lost 6 guns
124	lost 6 guns

VIII

37 (nearly both wagon lines)	550
61 (all with battery)	648
65	840

Third Division:—

XXIII

107 (about)	800 lost 2 guns
108	697 lost 2 guns
109 (about)	1,000[2]

Fourth Division. No record.

It is hoped that officers will be able to supply information to complete the ammunition expenditure of each battery, it will be extremely interesting and valuable.

---

1. Nearly 15 full wagons.

2. 109 could certainly have fired more; but early in the day, the B.C. had been warned that he was to be careful of ammunition.

NOTE.

At Waterloo, 18 June, 1815, Captain Sandham's Field Brigade R.A., (now 7 R.F.A.) fired 1,100 rounds during the Battle from its six muzzle-loading 9 pdrs. On the same day Major Whinyates' IInd Rocket Troop, R.H.A., fired 560 rounds from its six light 6 pdrs., and 52 rockets. Our 78 guns on this day fired nearly 10,000 rounds.[3]

In the decisive battle of Gravelotte, 18 Aug. 1870, the 456 French guns only fired 35,000 rounds, although one Battery belonging to the IV Corps fired 1,380 during the action.[4]

On the German side in the same battle the 616 guns, actually engaged, fired 34,628 common shell, 196 shrapnel, and 20 canister, total 34,844 rounds. The maximum fired by any one battery was 1,104 rounds.[5]

At Weissenburg, 4 Aug., 1870, the 90 German guns, actually engaged, fired only 1380 common shell and 19 shrapnel, total 1399 rounds. The maximum fired by any one battery was 200 rounds.[6] I cannot ascertain the expenditure of ammunition by the French artillery (12 guns) in this action.

At Magersfontein, 11 December 1899, our field batteries expended an average of 1,000 rounds apiece, and "G" R.H.A. fired 1,163 rounds.[7] Considering that the action lasted eleven hours, this amount cannot be regarded as excessive.

During this war, particularly since the advent of trench warfare, the rate has risen steadily. In 1916, 3,000 rounds in a day from an 18 pdr. battery was not unknown; whilst in 1917, even 4,000 has been surpassed.

Unfortunately batteries no longer keep diaries and this information is exceedingly hard to find in brigade diaries. Statements from battery officers of any excessive daily expenditure would be most acceptable for record purposes.

---

3. *The British Artillery at Waterloo*, by Captain Becke. *Journal, R.A. Institution*, Vol. XXXIV.

4. *Guerre de 1810-71*, III, (*Documents*). (Paris, 1905).

5. *German Artillery in 1870-71*. (1873), by Captain (later Lieut.-Colonel) Hime. R.A.; also the *Note* on the same published in Aug. 1873.

6. German artillery in 1870-71, (1873), by Captain (later Lieut.-Colonel) Hime, R.A., also the *Note* on the same published in August, 1873.

7. *Official History of the War in South Africa.*

An Artillery Officer on the Effects of the Battle

Brigadier-General C. De Sausmarez. C.B., C.M.G., D.S.O.,

An interesting narrative of the stand made at Le Cateau by General Sir Horace Smith-Dorrien is included in the January issue of the *Journal of the Royal Artillery*. The writer is Brigadier-General C. De Sausmarez. C.B., C.M.G., D.S.O., who commanded a heavy battery at Le Cateau. and who shows in a new light the part played by that action in destroying the effective development of the German plan of campaign. The narrative refers to the leading article in *The Times* on Sir Horace Smith-Dorrien's book which, he says, rightly drew attention to the fact that Lord Ypres, by countenancing the decision of the IInd. Corps commander to stand and fight, shared with him the credit of crippling the German pursuit. Brigadier-General de Sausmarez. in dealing with the possibilities had the stand not been made, says:—

The German plan of advancing in numerous columns, attacking wherever opposition was met and never stopping, must have formed part of the military creed of all ranks from general to private. They were taught to believe that this was the only sure road to victory. With their numbers, their iron discipline, the bravery and physical fitness of their troops, they came near to justifying their creed. It is pleasant to think that they were taught at this early stage that the British Army of 1914 was good enough to thwart them, and we may be thankful that Sir John French's 'Great Subordinate' recognized this important fact and utilised his knowledge by standing up to them and striking them a crippling blow, instead of retiring with those of his troops who could march, and leaving the remainder to their fate.

The detail contained in the articles is a valuable addition to the data concerning Le Cateau and supports the view taken in the official history of the operations that the decision to stand and fight had very important consequences, and led to the ultimate abandonment of the original German offensive which, but for Le Cateau, might have succeeded.

It is of course a mistake to dogmatise concerning the consequences of a supposititious happening. but it is not unreasonable to assume that the Battle of the Marne would not m these supposititious circumstances have been the victory for the Allies, which in truth was the case The German sledge-hammer plan of moving ruthlessly forward, each column attacking and knocking out everything that withstood it, came perilously near to success as it was but the machine was thrown out of gear by the blow it received at Le Cateau. which was one of the chief causes of the war not being won by the Germans off-hand, 'according to plan.' Had this blow not been dealt and had the German machine not been thereby thrown out of gear, it is unpleasant even to contemplate what might have happened. That all the tactical dispositions for the battle were perfect and could not have been improved upon, no one who has studied the subject seriously could possibly assert: but it is contended that the strategical conception of the battle was the correct one, and that General Sir Horace Smith-Dorrien made a great and light decision when he determined to stand and fight.

The Stand at Le Cateau, 26th August, 1914

By Brig.-General C. De Sausmarez, C.B., C.M.G., D.S.O.

Although much about this subject has been written, more and more will probably be added as time goes by. There are several reasons for this, of which the chief is that students of military history are beginning to know the details of the 1914 campaign; and the more thoroughly conversant the man of average intelligence becomes with the facts as narrated by the historian, made clearer by a study, map in hand, of the actual ground, the more does he speculate as to the reasons for such and such a decision and the more severe are his mental strictures on some apparent failure to grasp an opportunity or seeming neglect of an elementary principle in minor tactics. He is apt, in his accumulated knowledge of historical facts, to regard the commander on the spot as having been as fully acquainted with every item as he is himself and to judge him accordingly.

Regarding the question whether General Sir Horace Smith-Dorrien's[1] decision was justified or not, some will come to one conclusion and some to another, while others will hover between the two. The opinion of some officer who was with the I Corps may carry weight, hinting that the stand was unnecessary, pointing to the ease with which the I Corps slipped away, and asking why the remainder of the force could not do the same. Or possibly another officer of the I Corps will create quite a different impression by saying, "As we marched off and got away, we did feel grateful to those fellows for covering our retreat so splendidly." Both of these divergent opinions have actually been expressed by distinguished officers who fought in the

---

1. Smith-Dorrien: Isandlwhana to the Great War by Horace Smith-Dorrien is also published by Leonaur.

121

I Corps in the summer of 1914. Curiously enough, neither of them give a true picture of what actually occurred.

To an officer of the II Corps who had the privilege of fighting under General Sir Horace Smith-Dorrien this subject has always been of the keenest interest, any available writing thereon in the public press or elsewhere having been eagerly read. There was a fine leading article in the *Times*, when that newspaper published the advanced extracts from the general's book which dealt with Le Cateau and other incidents of his career in France. This article drew attention—and rightly—to the fact that the late Lord Ypres by countenancing the decision of his "great subordinate" to stand and fight, shared with him the credit of crippling the German pursuit.

On the other hand, in a review of the book in the *Sunday Times*, Mr. Herbert Sidebotham asserts that the opinion that "the battle was unnecessary, a waste of life, and dangerous to the safety of the army" will be "generally accepted." One wonders how and whence this writer got this view and how much real study he has given to the subject. He may be a most distinguished journalist, indeed a perfect archangel of journalism, but it is remarkable how *angels will sometimes rush in where the ordinary fool would fear to tread*. Why, it will be asked, does not the present writer fear to tread that path, even though it be in an angel's footsteps? Perhaps it is because his folly is extraordinary.

The following brief attempt to deal with a thorny subject, after a study of Brigadier-General Edmonds' Official History and Major A. F. Becke's book entitled *The Royal Regiment of Artillery at Le Cateau*, is made by one who saw something of the condition of the troops on the 25th August, 1914, who had the honour of fighting in the battle on the 26th, and who has lately had the great advantage of attending a most interesting and instructive staff tour on the battlefield.

With regard to the two books above mentioned the Official History is invaluable to anyone who is trying to master all the facts. It is probably far more interesting to the real student than to the casual reader, who cannot be bothered with so much detail. Some gifted people have marvellous memories, but the average man must read and re-read with the map General Edmonds' account of the events leading up to any one battle, of the battle itself and of its immediate consequences. Tackled in this fashion the book is not only invaluable as an instructional guide but of absorbing interest.

Major Becke's is a wonderful book, published as it was at the beginning of 1919, two months after the armistice. Not only do we find a clear narrative and sound and instructive comments, but parts of the book form an epic. At first sight we are inclined to grumble at the number and length of the footnotes, but when fairly launched we clamour for more and more footnotes, such as those which portray the deeds of the field batteries of the 5th Division. Although in the light of subsequent information we may not agree with one or two of the deductions made by the author, we cannot but admire a treatise, on the whole so sound and well-reasoned. He is perhaps a little hard on von Kluck when he says that he was merely a *bon général ordinaire*.

It must be remembered that this general was himself a subordinate; that he was misled by a report from the German Supreme Command as to the direction of the British Line of Communications; that information to be gleaned from air reconnaissance was comparatively meagre at that early stage; and that he had immediately opposed to him in the British commander-in-chief and his two corps commanders three tried leaders of a fighting type as great as that of the men whom they commanded. The wonderful march performed by the German First Army, interrupted as it was by severe fighting, seems proof in itself that von Kluck was a leader of a high order. It is hardly correct that he did not attempt to organise a pursuit after Le Cateau.

A considerable portion of his pursuing troops, the 2nd Cavalry Division and part of the 9th Cavalry Division, of von der Marwitz's II Cavalry Corps, had been badly handled by the British 4th Division on the 26th August and were hardly fit to move that day; the remainder of this corps were opposed to, though not severely engaged with, the British 3rd Division in the centre, von Kluck's orders for the 27th were that the II Cavalry Corps should advance in front of the German right flank and hinder the British retreat. Had he had cavalry available to intervene on the British right flank the story of Le Cateau might have had a less successful ending. At about 3 p.m. German cavalry were actually seen from one of our battery observing posts, moving south on the high ground west of Landrecies. The visibility was not good, there were other pressing affairs of the moment which prevented anything like an accurate computation of the numbers, but it is estimated that there was at least a regiment and possibly a brigade. To whom did they belong? They may have been the cavalry of the German III or IV Corps, and probably the role assigned to them by their corps commander was to watch the western flank.

To return to Mr. Sidebotham; this writer goes on to say:

After the Mons front had been abandoned owing to the defeat of the French right, the only thing to be done was to retreat to the new front with as little delay and loss as possible. Haig did it, and Smith-Dorrien, although his position was the more dangerous, might have done it too.

So far as these two generals knew up to a fairly late hour of the afternoon of the 25th, the portion of the "new front" to be held by the B.E.F. was the "Cambrai—Le Cateau" position. At a little after 3 p.m. on the 25th the G.O.C. I Corps received at Landrecies a message from G.H.Q., asking when he could take up his allotted portion of this position, Inchy to St. Benin. His troops were then for the most part still on the march on the east of the Forêt de Mormal. The G.O.C. II Corps, knowing that the I Corps was delayed, issued instructions for the temporary occupation (in addition to his own front) of a portion of the front destined to be occupied by the I Corps, and one and a half battalions of the 14th Infantry Brigade which was rear guard of the 5th Division, were sent to the east of Le Cateau after they had come in at 6.30 p.m. At that time the 7th Infantry Brigade (rear guard of the 3rd Division) and the 4th Division (of which the bulk of the infantry and one brigade of artillery, having detrained at Le Cateau on the 24th, had been sent by G.H.Q. to the neighbourhood of Solesmes to cover the retirement of the II Corps) were still a long way off, fighting, or in a position to fight, a delaying action some miles to the west of the Forêt de Mormal.

The first indications of a change of plan were received by the G.O.C. I Corps through his senior general staff officer, who had motored from G.H.Q. with instructions that his command should march, the 1st Division to St. Martin, 5 miles south of Le Cateau, the 2nd to Bazuel, 2 miles S.E. of that town. He issued orders for the march to begin at 2 a.m. on the 26th. The G.O.C. II Corps, in a private note timed 3.45 p.m. from the deputy chief of the general staff, was told that orders for a further retirement would reach him later.

It was not till a considerably later hour that the I Corps received the written order to continue the retirement on the 26th, and this operation order, though it indicated the same south-westerly direction as did the instructions received through the senior general staff officer, laid down that the retirement of the I Corps should be carried out as far as Busigny, 7 miles S.S.W. of Le Cateau.

At the time this order was received the 5th Infantry Brigade of the 2nd Division, which eventually passed the night of the 25th-26th at Noyelles, had not even then arrived near its destination. The 4th (Guards) and 6th Infantry Brigade (both of the 2nd Division) had arrived at Landrecies and Maroilles respectively. The 1st Division was in billets to the east, at Dompierre, Marbaix and Le Grand Fayt. In the same operation order G.H.Q. directed that the II Corps should retire to Beaurevoir (exclusive), Prémont and La Sabliere, and the 4th Division to Beaurevoir and Le Catelet. This order reached the G.O.C. II Corps at 9 p.m., and he issued orders accordingly that the transport should march at 4 a.m. and the main bodies at 7 a.m. on the 26th. The 7th Infantry Brigade, with the brigade of artillery which also belonged to the 3rd Divisional rearguard, had not even then arrived in bivouac. The 4th Division were still further behind.

The evening and night of the 25th-26th were disturbing for the I Corps, as fighting developed between a detachment of the 6th Infantry Brigade and a small mixed force of the enemy a mile or more to the N.W. of Maroilles, which petered out soon after dark; and between the 4th (Guards) Brigade and a larger enemy force just N.W. of Landrecies, which lasted until past midnight. The appreciation of the situation at I Corps Headquarters seems, very naturally, to have been that the enemy was attempting to penetrate between the British I and II Corps, that the left flank of the I Corps was already threatened, and that an attack from the west and northwest was to be expected in the morning. Had the G.O.C. been acquainted with the facts that are now known to us, this appreciation would have been very different.

We now know that the troops near Maroilles belonged to the German III Corps who had orders to march next morning *via* Landrecies (north)—Le Cateau to Maretz, with a view to the envelopment of the British right flank on the Le Cateau position; and that those near Landrecies belonged to the 7th Division of the German IV Corps who had orders to march to Montay with a view to striking the right centre of the British Army, and holding it to its ground. In both cases the contact was fortuitous, the Germans having merely spread themselves to obtain billeting room. The first contact at Landrecies seems to have been with the escort of some regimental transport which had been ordered to pass the column in order to get into billets.

Of course none of these details were known at Le Grand Fayt, where our I Corps Headquarters were spending the night. They merely had information of contact with the pursuing enemy at two points on a line running roughly N.E. to S.W. These indications were ominous and it must have looked as if an attack against the left flank were to be expected from the German First Army, sufficiently big to hold the British I Army Corps until the Second German Army should come down like a wolf on the fold from the north. If this appreciation of the situation had been correct, then it would have been rash to attempt to march to the S.W., across the front of the enemy's attack from the N.W.

It is not definitely known whether the appreciation above indicated was actually made at Le Grand Fayt on the night of the 25th-26th, but if (as seems most natural and probable) it was, it accounts for the retreat of the I Corps being carried out in a southerly direction to Etreux instead of a S.W. direction to Busigny as ordered by G.H.Q. Had the Germans not "blundered on to" them (to use Major Becke's expression) near Maroilles and Landrecies, the I Corps would probably have marched at 2 a.m. to Busigny; and, so far as can be gathered from the Official History, it seems most probable that the whole of the 2nd Division, from Noyelles, Maroilles and Landrecies, would have got clear as easily to the S.W. *via* Ors or Catillon, as did in fact the 4th (Guards) Brigade, retiring due S. in the very early morning from Landrecies.

No doubt Sir Horace Smith-Dorrien expected that the I Corps would attempt to retire to Busigny, as ordered by G.H.Q., and he feared for their fate if he did not stand to cover their retirement.

The dispositions of the I Corps for the 26th were briefly as follows. The 1st Division took up a position near Favril and on its left flank the 4th (Guards) Brigade, starting before dawn, retired due south without molestation. The 5th and 6th Infantry Brigades retired by the right flank, and owing to congestion on the road the 5th Infantry Brigade was very late. The retirement of the 1st Division began at 1 p.m., actually before the 5th Infantry Brigade had passed them, but they did not reach their billets at Fesmy and Oisy till 10 p.m. The 5th Infantry Brigade eventually halted for the night at Barzy, 5 miles N.E. of the bulk of the 2nd Division at Etreux.

So great was the delay in the retirement of the 5th Infantry Brigade that the rear-guard, the 2/Connaught Rangers, was actually engaged with troops of the German I Cavalry Corps and Second Army, who made prisoners of about 100 of our men. This incident gives some indication of what might have happened had the German First Army attacked our I Corps in flank from the west. Supposing, for the moment, that they had actually done so, what would have been the fate of the I Corps? General Haig would have been compelled in effect to stand and fight; he might have halted the 4th Guards Brigade on its march southwards, and used it in a counter-attack to prevent envelopment.

We may be sure that the I Corps would have put up as good a fight as did Sir Horace Smith-Dorrien's command, but the odds against them would have been terrific, with the German First Army holding them until the Second Army should arrive from the north, von Richthofen's cavalry being employed, perhaps, in getting round to their rear by the right flank. The odds against General Smith-Dorrien were big enough, but small compared to those with which General Haig would have had to contend, had the German First Army attacked his command instead of General Smith-Dorrien's.

If the II Corps, 4th Division and cavalry had retired in accordance with the orders of G.H.Q., the I Corps would in all probability have ceased to exist. Would the II Corps commander then have received a pat on the back from some kind journalist, the I Corps commander being duly censured for not getting back to the "new position"?

The case of the I Corps would not have been so hopeless with the Le Cateau position held, because a German attack from the west would perforce have been half-hearted, and the I Corps, though perhaps badly crippled, would have contrived to avoid envelopment.

Had Sir H. Smith-Dorrien's troops been fresh, unwearied and free from battle casualties, it is not unlikely that G.H.Q. would have ordered him to cover the retirement of the I Corps, without any suggestion on his part that he should do so. It must, however, have been known at G.H.Q. that his troops had had severe fighting on the 24th, that their casualties had been large, that they had had little rest for five days, and that they were probably short of food. The operation order directing both corps to march S.W. was probably drafted with the intention of keeping the two corps as near together as possible.

It said little or nothing about co-operation, though no doubt the hope was that by marching on parallel routes at no great distance from one another, one corps would be able to help the other should the need arise. Whether the consideration of the wearying and trying conditions imposed on the II Corps, their casualties, their constant fighting and marching, induced G.H.Q. to ask nothing further of them we do not know, but we do know that these very conditions, coupled with the fact that the enemy were on their heels, were the compelling reason for the stand made at Le Cateau.

In the early morning of the 25th, the day before the battle, it happened that the 108th Heavy Battery was a long way back in the 5th Divisional Column, marching down the Roman Road to the west of the Forêt de Mormal. Orders had been issued for a unit of the 14th Infantry Brigade to halt and go back on their tracks to reinforce the rear-guard or relieve the rear party. As they streamed past the battery it was pitiful to see the men's faces, dirty, starved of food and rest, and desperate at the idea of more marching to be done and ground already covered once to be covered again and yet again. To add to their misery the weather was extremely sultry and the forest shut out any breeze there might have been.

An infantry officer informed the battery commander that he had been ordered to hand over a platoon as escort to the battery, and added that the men were dead-beat and faint from want of food. "If you give them something to eat," he said, "they'll fight damned well for you, provided they haven't to move far." Fortunately, the battery had helped itself on the previous day to biscuits and bully as well as oats from a deserted supply dump, and the men were only too glad to give a square meal to their comrades, who, loaded with rifle and pack, and desperately hungry and tired, were in a bad plight. But the infantry officer's words were true, and what is more his description was typical of most of the infantry.

There was the situation in a nutshell; they were ready to go on till they dropped, but were in imminent danger of dropping; give them a chance to halt and have a bit of food, and they would cheerfully fight while they rested. And this was the morning of the day before the battle, and they had many weary miles to cover before reaching their bivouacs on the Le Cateau position. If an infantry officer who fought at Le Cateau is consulted on the subject, he will almost certainly say that his men could not have continued the retreat in the early morning of the 26th; that they had more than a little sting left in them while they rested their legs in battle during that day, the Germans would doubtless confirm.

We know from the Official History and from his own account that when General Smith-Dorrien between 2 and 3 a.m. on the 26th considered the condition of his infantry and the fact that several of the II Corps units, and practically the whole of the infantry and some of the artillery of the 4th Division had not even then arrived in bivouac, he was faced with a very difficult problem. How could he best carry out the orders received from G.H.Q., which, as we w have seen above, were to retire to Beaurevoir and La Sabliere? To retire at once, or as soon as those troops who were on the position could be got ready, was unthinkable. How could those who were still wending their way to the position with the enemy on their heels be left behind? And yet the cavalry commander told him that unless he could get on the move at once it would be necessary to fight next day, the cavalry being too much scattered and their horses too beat for them to be of the smallest value in covering the retirement of the force.

He had therefore one of two choices left to him, either to act in accordance with the orders he had already issued, but giving a bigger proportion of artillery to his rearguards, or to fight with his whole force in the hope of striking the enemy such a blow as would cripple their pursuit.

The orders that he had already issued detailed one infantry brigade and two artillery brigades per division, with the cyclist company and divisional squadron, as rearguards. (So far as concerned the 5th Division each of the three artillery brigades was affiliated to an infantry brigade, and the howitzer brigade and the heavy battery were to be under the control of the C.R.A. It seems therefore as if the intention was that the two artillery brigades who should form part of the rearguard were the 18 pr. brigade, affiliated to the 13th Infantry Brigade (which was detailed for rear-guard duty), and the howitzer brigade, the heavy battery being added; whilst the other two 18 pr. brigades were also in a position to act should the infantry brigade to which they were affiliated be compelled to fight before leaving the position. It was evidently contemplated by the G.O.C. 5th Division that a fight might be necessary before evacuating any part of the line.)

The first alternative, to leave a brigade of infantry per division and the bulk of his artillery to cover the retirement of the remainder of the force, was (if it ever occurred to him) rejected by Sir Horace Smith-Dorrien, and he decided on the second alternative, to fight with his whole force. Let us try to picture what would have happened if the first alternative had been adopted.

Dealing first with the right flank the action would have begun in the same manner, and one and a half battalions of the 14th Infantry Brigade, who were preparing to march off from Le Cateau would have been caught in exactly the same unfortunate way as actually happened. They and the remainder of the 14th Infantry Brigade would have eventually retired, probably with considerable casualties from artillery fire; the number of stragglers would have been large. The 15th

Infantry Brigade would have retired, no doubt with fewer casualties, for the Germans did not attack them seriously in the early part of the day. The 13th Infantry Brigade which was in the centre of the 5th Division would have been isolated with strong enemy forces attacking their front and right flank. Their fate would probably have been annihilation.

Turning to the left of the line, the whole of the 4th Division would have perforce been engaged at the beginning of the action, for the infantry had not long arrived on the position from Solesmes before they were attacked by German cavalry, horse artillery and *jägers*. If the two brigades had marched off, the German cavalry would quite possibly have got round to the rear of the remaining brigade which would have been mopped up by the German IV Reserve Corps on its arrival. They would have learnt that the true direction of the British retreat was to the south rather than to the west, and von Kluck's wrong impression would have been removed.

It is possible that the rearguard brigade of the 3rd Division in the centre would have made good their retreat, but not without serious loss. At least one of the other two brigades would have lost fairly heavily. The number of stragglers throughout the whole force would have been very large.

Taking it all round we may be sure that the infantry casualties alone would have been as great, if not greater, than 8000, the approximate total number which occurred in the actual battle. It is possible that the loss in guns would have been trifling, or at all events much less than the actual loss.

As regards the Germans, we know that their casualties were very heavy. Our infantry fully maintained, as they did at Mons, their 600-year old reputation as individual marksmen. If our force had been deprived of two thirds of its infantry strength the German casualties would have been insignificant compared to those which they actually suffered. They were so badly hammered that the First Army lost its grip of the B.E.F. and never regained it. With only one-third of the rifle power against them this would not have been the case. Instead of reeling from the blow inflicted on them they would have been in a position not merely to move forward, groping, after they had recovered from the shock, but to maintain a vigorous pursuit and to compel the II Corps and 4th Division to stand and fight before they had crossed the Oise.

It is of course a mistake to dogmatise concerning the consequences of a suppositious happening, but it is not unreasonable to assume that the Battle of the Marne would not in these suppositious circumstances have been the victory for the Allies, which in truth was the case. The German sledge-hammer plan of moving ruthlessly forward, each column attacking and knocking out everything that withstood it, came perilously near to success as it was, but the machine was thrown out of gear by the blow it received at Le Cateau, which was one of the chief causes of the war not being won by the Germans off-hand, "according to plan." Had this blow not been dealt and had the German machine not been thereby thrown out of gear, it is unpleasant even to contemplate what might have happened.

That all the tactical dispositions for the battle were perfect and could not have been improved upon, no one who has studied the subject seriously could possibly assert; but it is contended that the strategical conception of the battle was the correct one, and that General Sir Horace Smith-Dorrien made a great and right decision, when he determined to stand and fight.

It was owing to force of circumstances that this decision was made with so very little time to spare, and that the Germans were able to attack before the British troops on the right flank had received orders not to retire. It is difficult to see how orders could have been communicated more quickly. If, immediately after the corps commander announced his decision to stand and fight, a message had been sent to the G.O.C. 5th Division telling him to insure above all things that his troops on the right flank were ready—not to retire—but to fight a defensive battle, it is conceivable, but doubtful, that arrangements could have been made in time for the one and a half battalions who were on the east of Le Cateau to be in position covering that town, and for the remainder of the 14th Infantry Brigade to occupy a more suitable position than that which they actually took up.

It was, however, an inspiration which caused a later order, to the effect that there was in no circumstances to be a retirement, to be issued for communication to all units. This order, at all events so far as concerned the 5th Division, was so firmly impressed on all units that two of them, the 2/Suffolk Regiment and the 2/K.O.Y.L.I., sacrificed themselves for the remainder of the force.

When, in the early afternoon, it was decided to break off the action, the orders to retire, presumably owing to the fact that the abnormally heavy fire prevented any message getting through to them, failed to reach the two battalions named above. They saw other troops retiring, but in spite of this held their ground because nothing had reached them cancelling the previous order that there was to be no retirement. Anyone privileged to read the diary of Major (later Lieut.-Colonel) Peebles who, owing to the death of his C.O. and to the second in command being severely wounded, commanded the 2/Suffolk Regiment at the end, will learn a story of devoted heroism, which loses nothing from the simple language used in its telling. He apparently did not know that all units had had similar injunctions not to retire, and assumed accordingly that it was the intention that his battalion should be sacrificed. He, therefore (as did Lieut.-Colonel Bond who commanded the battalion of Yorkshire Light Infantry on the left of the Suffolk Regiment), calmly accepted the principle that it was "expedient that one man should die for the people."

They both assumed that their battalions were cast for this role, and unhesitatingly sacrificed them, and (incidentally) their own future prospects. They have some, consolation in knowing that their action was invaluable, and that though they missed all further chances of honour and advancement through being prisoners of war, their names should live longer in history than those of many who were more fortunate.

These are the two outstanding instances of what may be called "accidental rearguards," but there were other examples in the 3rd and 4th Divisions of detachments whom the order to retire never reached, and who fought on stoutly, and caused consternation and delay to the enemy. To one and all we owe our gratitude, but we must not forget to be thankful for the inspiration which caused the special order to be issued which forbade any retirement. Supposing that the decision to stand and fight had not been made, it is quite conceivable that owing to the local situation at their respective positions the two infantry brigades per division would not have retired at once, and that the battle would have actually begun as it did, with all the troops engaged. If they had not had the special order that there was to be no retirement, it would have been understood that the main object was to retreat and not to fight, and the blow given to the Germans would have been trifling compared to that which was actually struck.

It is interesting to speculate as to the probable effect on the battle, if the I Corps had carried out the orders of G.H.Q. and marched at 2 a.m. S.W. to Busigny, instead of retiring in a southerly direction. There seems every reason to believe that one or more Infantry Brigades with a quota of artillery would have arrived within two miles of Le Cateau

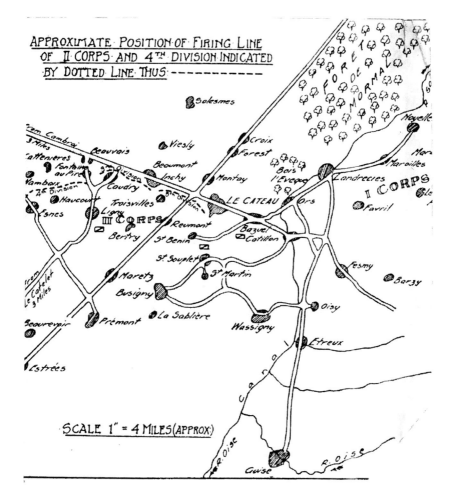

by 7.30 a.m., and would have been able to launch that counter-attack against the German left flank which General Smith-Dorrien longed, but owing to lack of reserves was not able, to deliver. Reinforcements would have kept coming in on his right, and Le Cateau might have been a tactical as well as a strategical victory for the British arms. It was indeed a misfortune that the Germans "blundered on to" the I Corps at Maroilles and Landrecies.

The German plan of advancing In numerous columns, attacking wherever opposition was met and never stopping, must have formed part of the military creed of all ranks from general to private. They were taught to believe that this was the only sure road to victory. With their numbers, their iron discipline, the bravery and physical fitness of their troops, they came near to justifying their creed. It is pleasant to think that they were taught at this early stage that the British Army of 1914 was good enough to thwart them, and we may be thankful that Sir John French's "Great Subordinate" recognised this important fact, and utilised his knowledge by standing up to them and striking them a crippling blow, instead of retiring with those of his troops who could march, and leaving the remainder to their fate.

Maps

OPERATIONS.
27 1914.

MAP I.

SCALE.

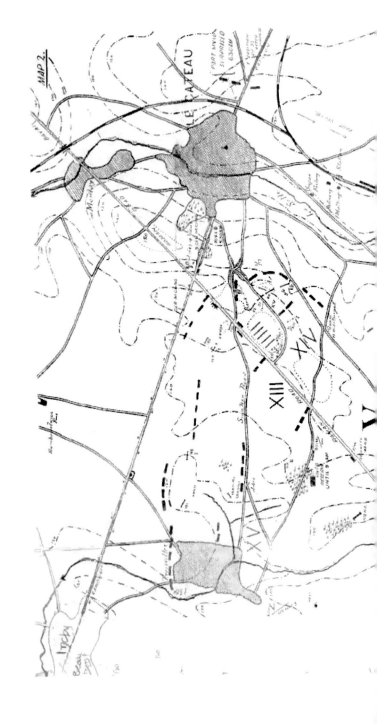

MAP 2.

R.A.v OLIVEN

St. ELI. 1914

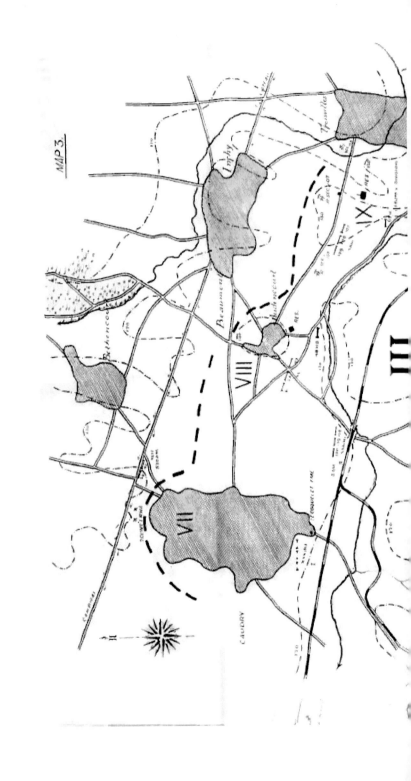

MAP 3

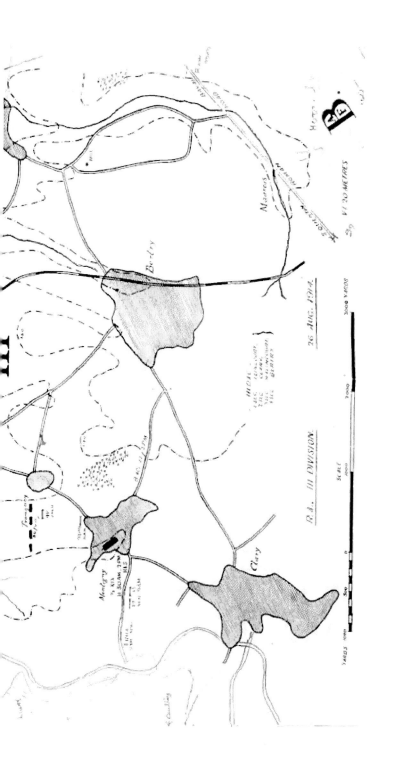

R.A. III DIVISION.   26 Aug. 1914.

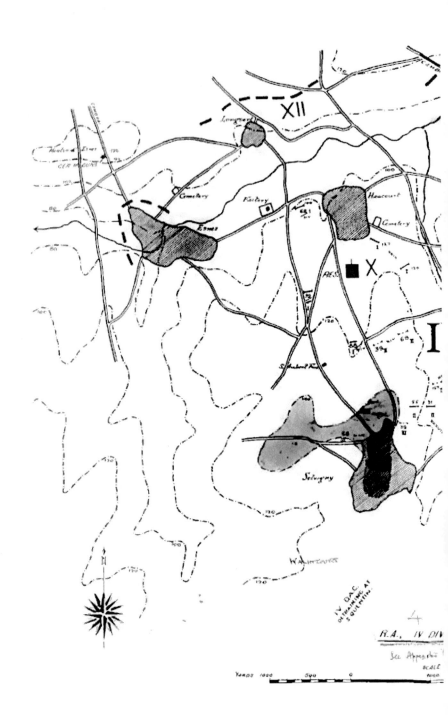

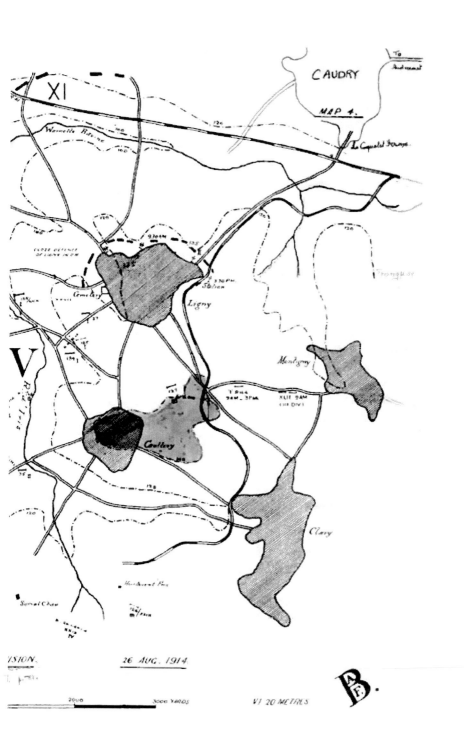

CAUDRY

MAP 4.

To Aut word

L. Copaled Grange.

XI

Warnelle Ravine

CLOSE DEFENCE
OF LIGNY IN 1914

9.30 A.M.

Cemetery

Ligny

5.30 P.M.
Selran

Montigny

Tronquoy

T B M.A
9 A.M., 3 P.M.

XLII 9A.M.
CIII DIV?

V

Cautery

Clary

Sorral Chau

ISION.   26 AUG. 1914

2000   3000 YARDS   VI 20 METRES $\mathcal{A}\mathcal{B}$.

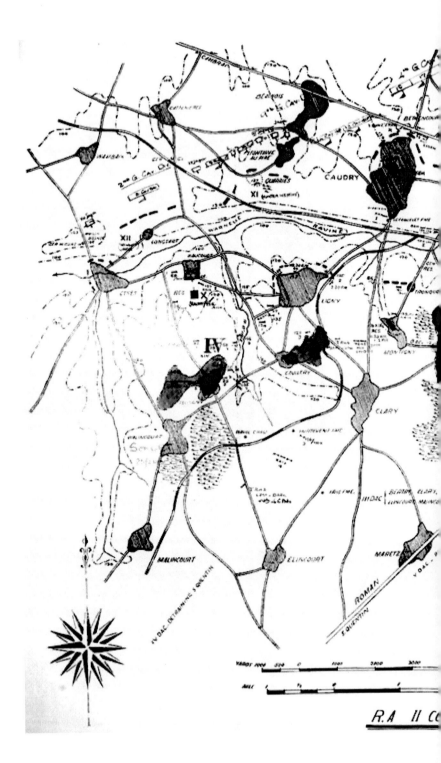

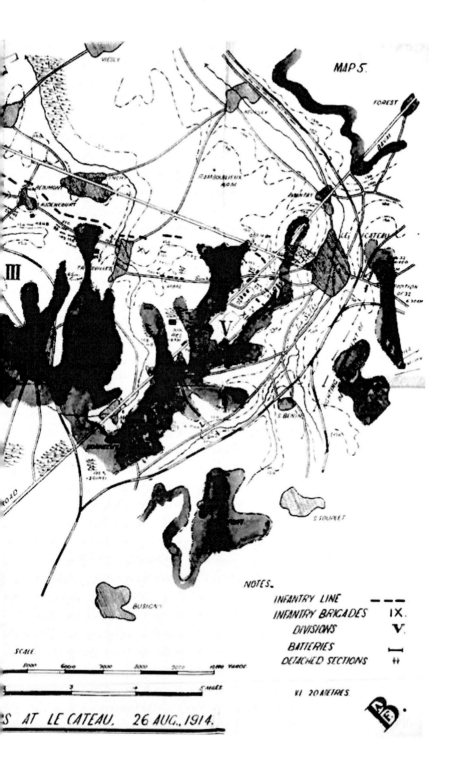

MAP 5.

FOREST

III

NOTES.

INFANTRY LINE   - - -
INFANTRY BRIGADES   IX.
DIVISIONS   V.
BATTERIES |—|
DETACHED SECTIONS   ++

VI 20 METRES.

SCALE

5000   6000   7000   8000   9000   10,000 YARDS

3   5 MILES

S AT LE CATEAU.   26 AUG., 1914.

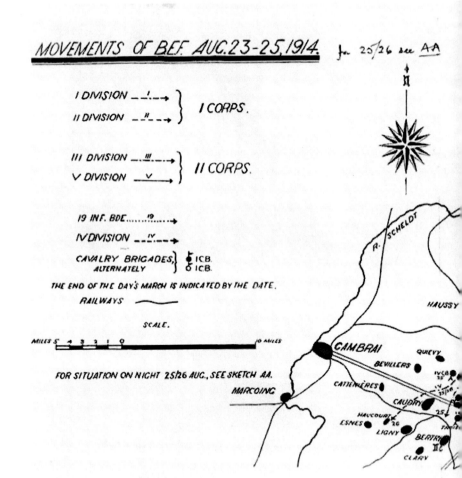

MOVEMENTS OF B.E.F. AUG.23-25,1914.

for 25/26 see AA

I DIVISION ___·__→
II DIVISION __"__→ } I CORPS.

III DIVISION ___"__→
V DIVISION ___ᵛ__→ } II CORPS.

19 INF. BDE...........¹⁹__→
IV DIVISION ___ᴵⱽ__→

CAVALRY BRIGADES, ⦵ I.C.B.
ALTERNATELY   ⦵ I.C.B.

THE END OF THE DAY'S MARCH IS INDICATED BY THE DATE.

RAILWAYS ———

SCALE.

MILES 5 4 3 2 1 0   10 MILES

FOR SITUATION ON NIGHT 25/26 AUG., SEE SKETCH AA.

R. SCHELDT

HAUSSY

CAMBRAI

QUIEVY

BEVILLERS

CATTENIÈRES

CAUDRY

MARCOING

HAUCOURT
ESNES   LIGNY

BERTRY

CLARY

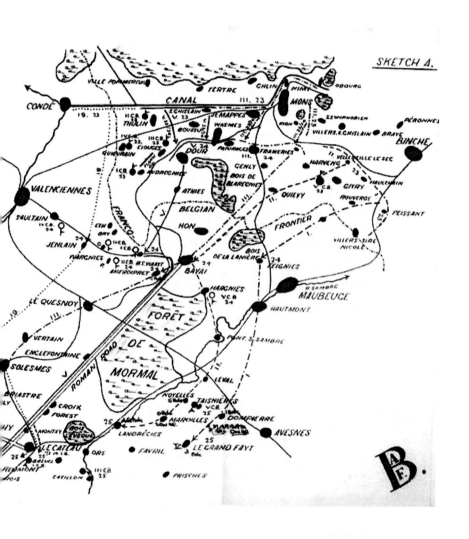

SKETCH A.

SITUATION OF B.E.F., NIGHT 25/26 AUG., 1914.

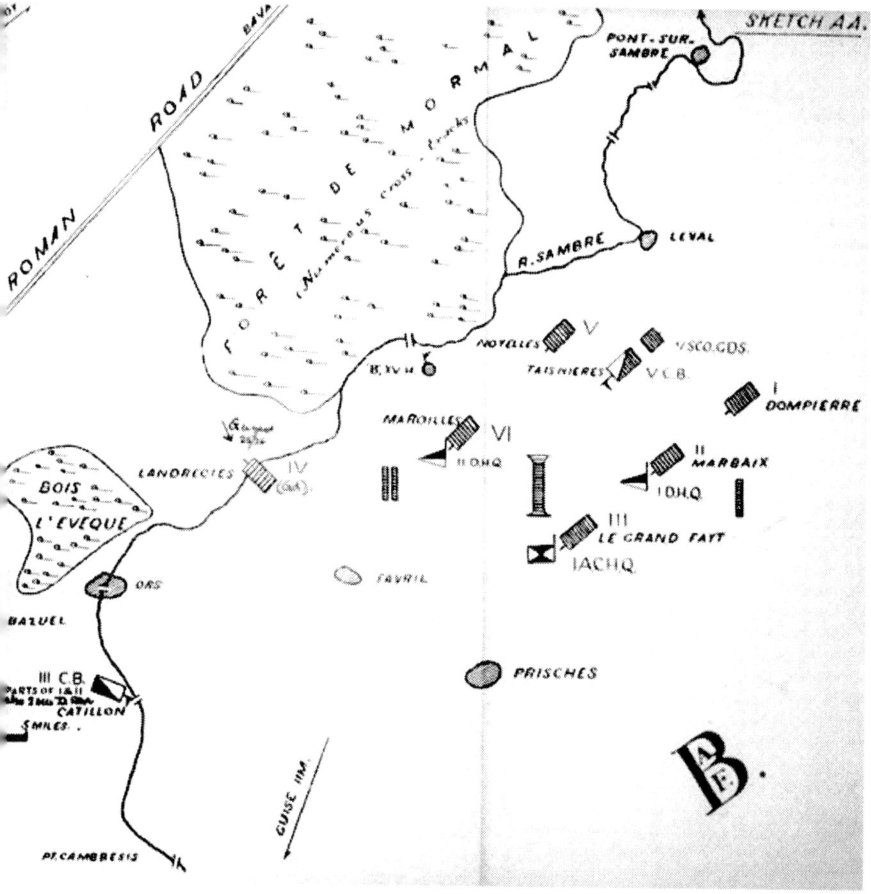

SKETCH A.A.

ROMAN ROAD

BAVA

FORET DE MORMAL

(Numerous cross roads)

PONT-SUR-SAMBRE

R. SAMBRE

LEVAL

NOTELLES

V

V SCO. GDS.

TAISNIERES

V.C.B.

B. XV H.

I DOMPIERRE

MAROILLES

VI

II D.H.Q.

II MARBAIX

I D.H.Q.

LANDRECIES

IV (G.H.)

BOIS L'EVEQUE

III LE GRAND FAYT

IA CHQ

FAVRIL

ORS

BAZUEL

PRISCHES

III C.B.

PARTS OF I & II

CATILLON

5 MILES.

B.

PT. CAMBRESIS

GUISE 11M.

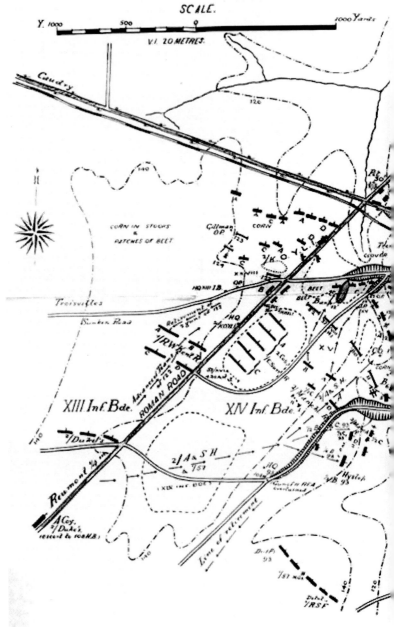

BRITISH RIGHT AT LE CATEAU.
AUG. 26, 1914.
SCALE.

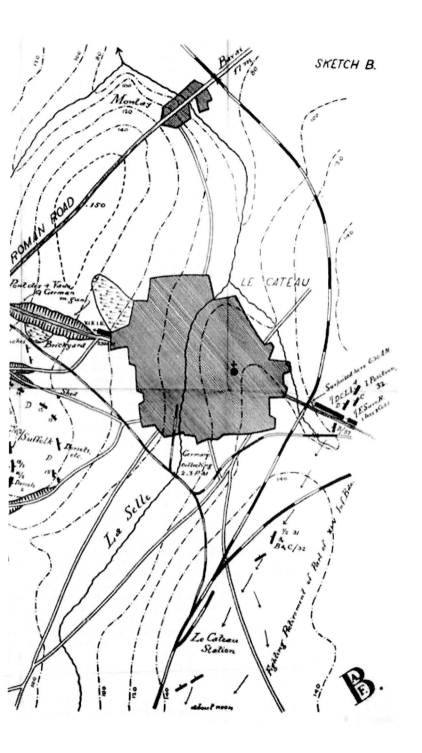

SKETCH B.

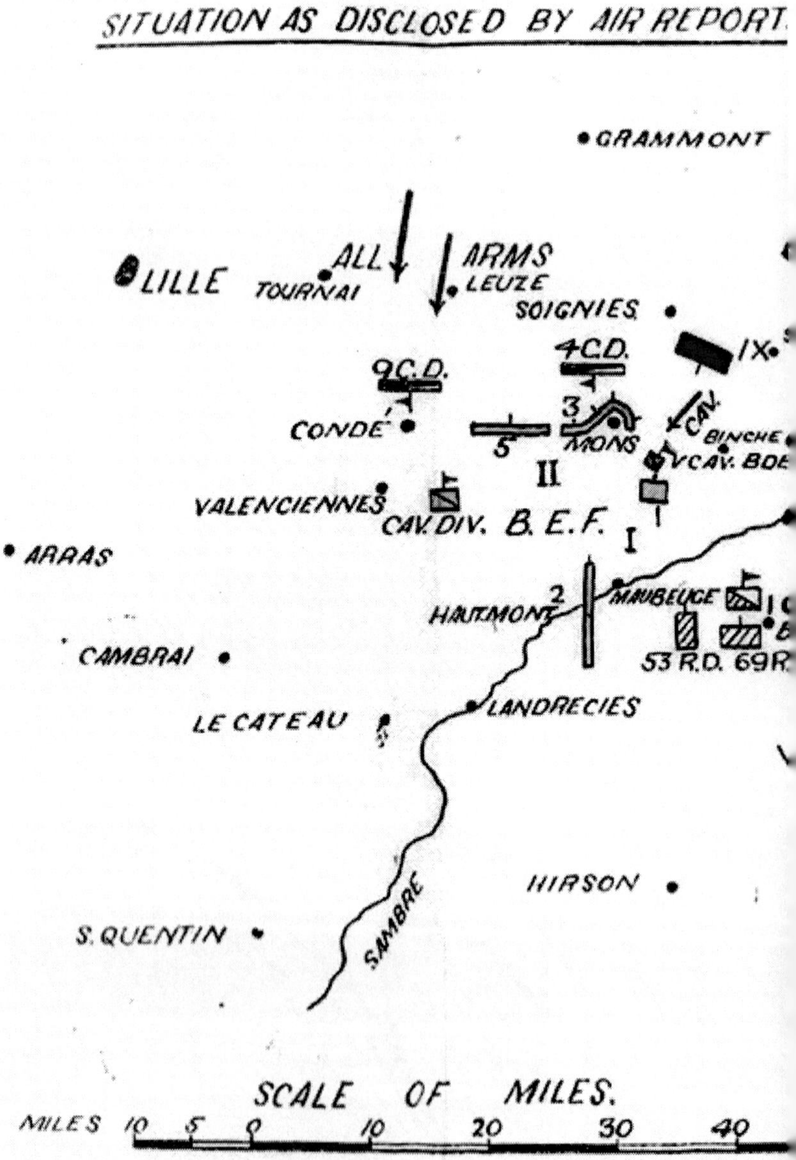

• GRAMMONT

⊙ LILLE

ALL ARMS

TOURNAI •

• LEUZE

SOIGNIES •

9C.D.

4C.D.

IX •

CONDÉ •

3

MONS

BINCHE •

5

V CAV. BDE.

II

VALENCIENNES

CAV. DIV. B.E.F. I

• ARRAS

HAUTMONT

2

MAUBEUGE

53 R.D. 69 R.

• CAMBRAI •

LE CATEAU

LANDRECIES

HIRSON •

SAMBRE

S. QUENTIN •

SCALE OF MILES.

MILES 10 5 0 10 20 30 40

SKETCH F.

S, NIGHT 22/23 AUG. 1914.

BRUSSELS

LIEGE

30,000
NIVELLES

ENEFFE

20,000

GEMBLOUX

GD.CAV.   GD.   X or VII

MEUSE   HUY

HARLEROI

AUVELAIS

NAMUR

THUIN   GERPINNES

XVIII

CINEY

AV.CORPS

DINANT

EAUMONT

D.

LESSE

GIVET

ANREZAC

ARMY

| B.E.F. |
| FRENCH. |
| GERMAN. |

ROCROI

MEUSE

MEZIERES

50 MILES

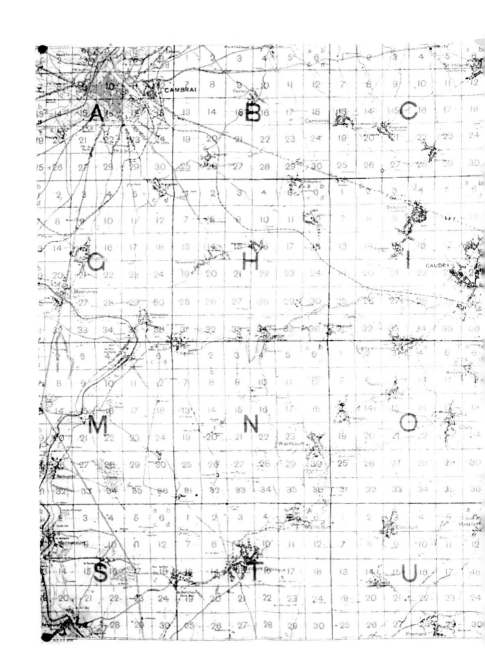

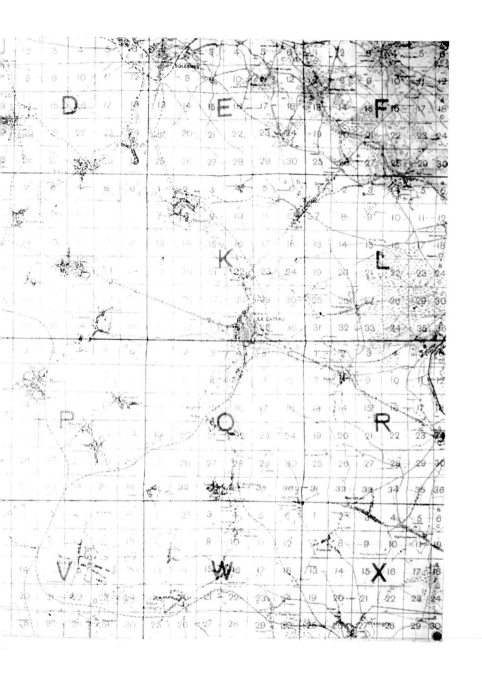

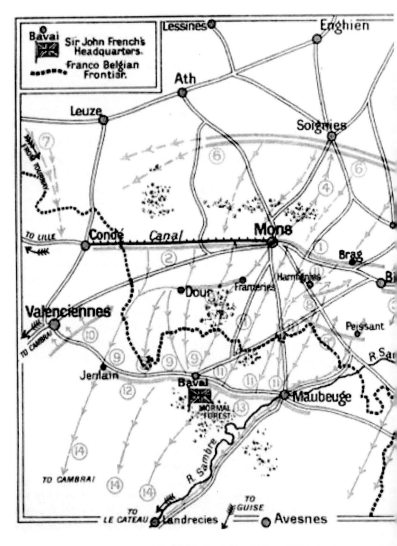

SKETCH OF THE CHIEF OPERATIONS NEAR MONS

(1) Original Position of 1st British Army Corps. (2) Original Position of
2nd British Army Corps. (3) Position of British Cavalry. (4) Line of the
early British Cavalry Reconnaissance. (5) Positions of the 5th French Army.
(5a) French Army Reserves. (6) German Forces. (7) German Turning Movement
from Tournay. (8) Demonstration of 2nd British Division towards Binche.

The above indications are ne

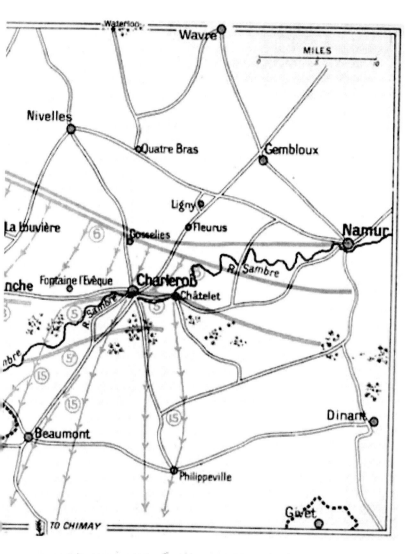

AND CHARLEROI—Based on Sir John French's Report

(8a) Supporting Position of 1st British Division.   (9) First Line of Retreat of
2nd British Corps.   (10) Covering Line of 19th British Infantry Brigade from
Valenciennes.   (11) Retreat of 1st British Corps.   (12) Position of 2nd Corps
after the First Retreat.   (13) Position of 1st Corps after the First Retreat.   (14) Subsequent British Retreat to the Cambrai-Le Cateau Line.   (15) French Retreat.
ccssarily only approximate ones.

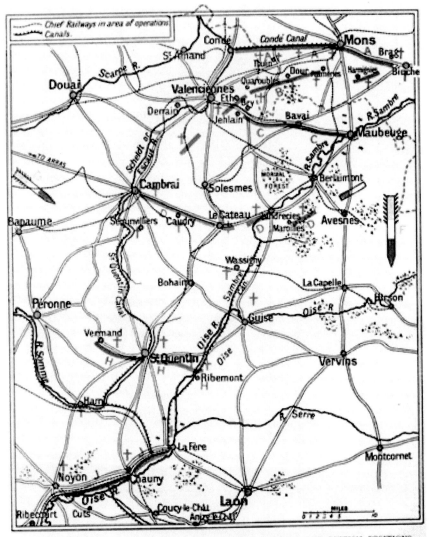

THE FIRST PHASE OF THE GREAT RETREAT· PLAN SHOWING THE BRITISH POSITIONS
FROM AUGUST 23 TO AUGUST 28, 1914

✝ Chief engagements during the Retreat ·········· Franco-Belgian Frontier.

A. British Positions at Mons, August 23.   B. Retiring Line of 2nd Army Corps, August 24.   C. British Lines,
evening, August 24.   D. British Lines, August 25-26.   E. Position of General Sordet's Cavalry, August 23-26.
F. General direction of French Retreat.   G. General d'Amade's movement from Arras to assist the British.   H. British
Lines, August 26-27.   J. British Lines, August 28.

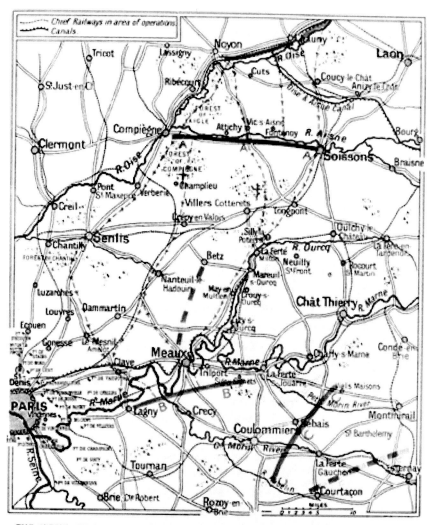

THE SECOND PHASE OF THE GREAT RETREAT: PLAN SHOWING THE BRITISH POSITIONS
FROM AUGUST 28 TO SEPTEMBER 6, 1914

The map also indicates the positions of the Allies and of the German Army under General von Kluck at the
beginning of the Battle of the Marne.

† Engagements on September 1.   Approximate British Lines of Retreat, August 28 to September 3.

A. British Lines, August 29.   B. British Lines, September 3.   C. British Lines, September 6.   D. Sixth French
        Army, September 6.   E. Von Kluck's Army, September 6.   F. Fifth French Army, September 6.

AUDENARDE

COURTRAI

B E

SCHELD RIV.

ST.OMER   HAZEBROUCK

ATH

LILLE   TOURNAI

F   BETHUNE

BATTLE LINE
ON AUG. 22. 1914

CONDÉ   MON

ST.POL   DOUAI   VALENCIENNES

R   BRITISH
ARMY

ARRAS   MAUE

DOULLENS   CAMBRAI   AVES

LE CATEAU

SOMME RIV.   PERONNE   OISE   RIV.

GUISE

AMIENS   VERMAND   ST.QUENTIN   VERVI

BATTLE LINE   RIBEMONT   SERRE   RIV.
ON AUG. 28. 1914   MARLE

ROYE   LA FERE

MONTDIDIER   CHAUNY   SISONI

LASSIGNY   NOYON   LAON

| GERMAN |
| FRENCH |
| ENGLISH |
| FORTS |
| MAIN R.R. |

COMPIÈGNE   AISNE RI

MILES   SOISSONS

0   5   10   15   R

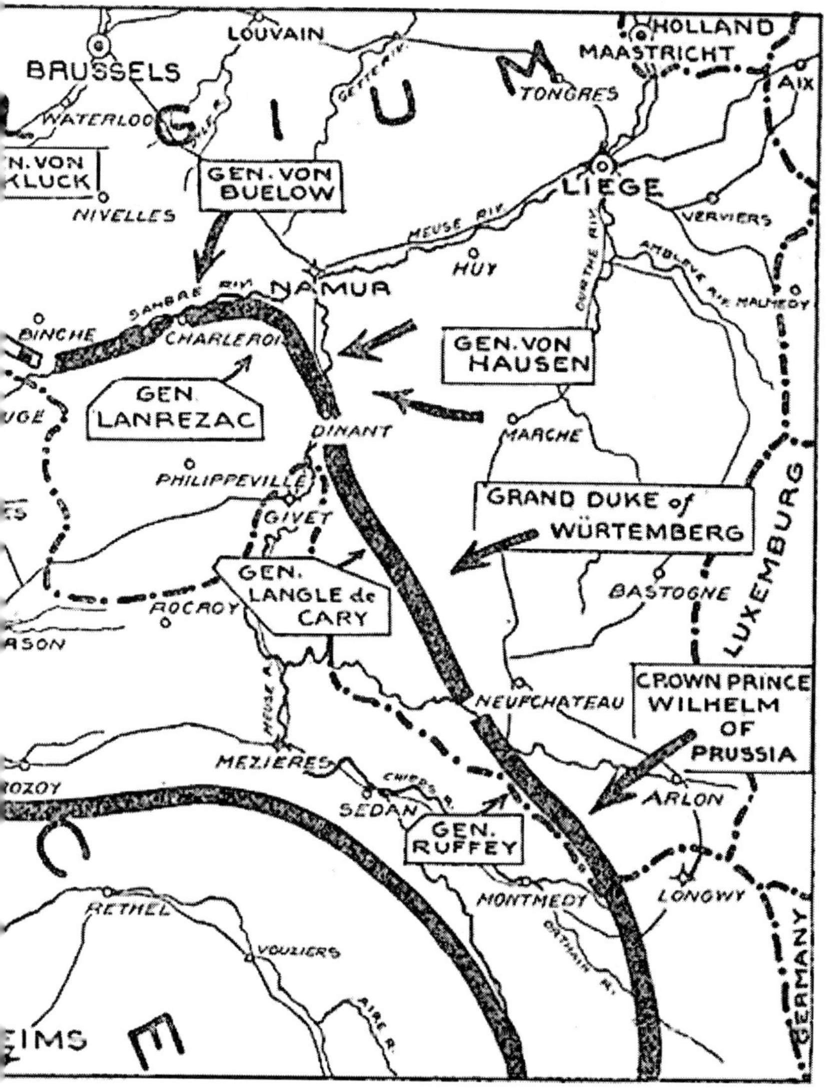

LOUVAIN
HOLLAND
MAASTRICHT
BRUSSELS
TONGRES
AIX
WATERLOO
N. VON
KLUCK
GEN. VON
BUELOW
LIEGE
NIVELLES
VERVIERS
MEUSE RIV.
HUY
NAMUR
MALMEDY
BINCHE
CHARLEROI
GEN. VON
HAUSEN
GEN.
LANREZAC
DINANT
MARCHE
PHILIPPEVILLE
GRAND DUKE of
WÜRTEMBERG
GIVET
GEN.
LANGLE de
CARY
BASTOGNE
ROCROY
LUXEMBURG
CROWN PRINCE
WILHELM
OF
PRUSSIA
NEUFCHATEAU
MEZIERES
SEDAN
ARLON
GEN.
RUFFEY
MONTMEDY
LONGWY
RETHEL
VOUZIERS
AIRE R.
GERMANY

LEONAUR

ALSO FROM LEONAUR
AVAILABLE IN SOFTCOVER OR HARDCOVER WITH DUST JACKET

OFFICERS & GENTLEMEN *by Peter Hawker & William Graham*—Two Accounts of British Officers During the Peninsula War: Officer of Light Dragoons by Peter Hawker & Campaign in Portugal and Spain by William Graham .

THE WALCHEREN EXPEDITION *by Anonymous*—The Experiences of a British Officer of the 81st Regt. During the Campaign in the Low Countries of 1809.

LADIES OF WATERLOO *by Charlotte A. Eaton, Magdalene de Lancey & Juana Smith*—The Experiences of Three Women During the Campaign of 1815: Waterloo Days by Charlotte A. Eaton, A Week at Waterloo by Magdalene de Lancey & Juana's Story by Juana Smith.

JOURNAL OF AN OFFICER IN THE KING'S GERMAN LEGION *by John Frederick Hering*—Recollections of Campaigning During the Napoleonic Wars.

JOURNAL OF AN ARMY SURGEON IN THE PENINSULAR WAR *by Charles Boutflower*—The Recollections of a British Army Medical Man on Campaign During the Napoleonic Wars.

ON CAMPAIGN WITH MOORE AND WELLINGTON *by Anthony Hamilton*—The Experiences of a Soldier of the 43rd Regiment During the Peninsular War.

THE ROAD TO AUSTERLITZ *by R. G. Burton*—Napoleon's Campaign of 1805.

SOLDIERS OF NAPOLEON *by A. J. Doisy De Villargennes & Arthur Chuquet*—The Experiences of the Men of the French First Empire: Under the Eagles by A. J. Doisy De Villargennes & Voices of 1812 by Arthur Chuquet .

INVASION OF FRANCE, 1814 *by F. W. O. Maycock*—The Final Battles of the Napoleonic First Empire.

LEIPZIG—A CONFLICT OF TITANS *by Frederic Shoberl*—A Personal Experience of the 'Battle of the Nations' During the Napoleonic Wars, October 14th-19th, 1813.

SLASHERS *by Charles Cadell*—The Campaigns of the 28th Regiment of Foot During the Napoleonic Wars by a Serving Officer.

BATTLE IMPERIAL *by Charles William Vane*—The Campaigns in Germany & France for the Defeat of Napoleon 1813-1814.

SWIFT & BOLD *by Gibbes Rigaud*—The 60th Rifles During the Peninsula War.